America, Taking Back Our Democrat Party

Jim Abel

www.yourdemocratparty.com

ISBN-10: 1460998928
EAN-13: 9781460998922

ACKNOWLEDGMENTS

I would like to acknowledge and thank my beautiful wife for being so patient with me as I have been working on this book, without her support, this book would not have been possible. I would also like to thank a few people who helped me with editing this work. To Debbie Schupp: thank you for your time. To Jarom my son: Thank you for your help and effort; I am so proud of you. To my father in-law, Doug Swift: You have great insight and wisdom, thank you for your help. This work is better because of you. To Sandi Madsen, thank you for your expertise and time, you have made this work complete, I owe you big time. I would like most of all to thank my parents and grandparents for teaching me the values of good government, conservatism and the history and Constitution of America.

CONTENTS

Preface and Introduction

I would like to say a few words as an introduction, mostly to explain why I came to write this book and to describe some of the political influences throughout my life. I consider myself a strong conservative and have been aligned with the Republican Party most of my life. I have read extensively from the writings of Dr. W. Cleon Skousen, perhaps one of our foremost authorities on our founding fathers and the Constitution of the United States of America. Many of my political views and knowledge of American history come from him and his books. For many years, I have been interested in politics and have been a watcher, as most Americans, of the Republican party and the Democrat party, one party considered to be conservative the other liberal. I have wondered how we came to have a two party system, how they had such different beliefs, and if these two parties have always believed the way they do? It is true; my desire was more to investigate the Democrat Party, as I did not know much about it. I also felt strongly that the Socialist leanings of this party are problematic for our country and our freedoms. My real question is: Has the Democrat party always been this way? I have found the answer to be, "No". History will show that the Democrat party was, in its birth and throughout much of its existence, very conservative. I have also wondered how to bring the party back in alignment with the American people. This is the point of this book. We must not let the American Democrat party die; after all, it is one of our greatest achievements. It is America's Party, America's first and oldest political party; it belongs to all of us. In days past it has served America well, but now it seems America serves it. We must take back our Democrat Party.

CHAPTER I

HISTORY

Before we can discuss how we take back our Democrat Party, it would be wise to review the history of this once great political movement. The Democratic party of the United States of America is one of, if not the oldest, political party still in existence today. The Democratic-Republican Party was started by Thomas Jefferson and a few others in the 1790's as a protest of the federal government's involvement in the affairs of the individual states and citizens.

Thomas Jefferson, James Madison, and other contemporaries of our founding fathers thought that the Federal Government was already becoming too powerful: and they believed it's encroachment on the rights of the states and citizens of America showed signs of danger for our nation. Thus the Democratic-Republican party was formed with Thomas Jefferson as its first president and a party platform of states' rights and limited federal government. The young party espoused loyalty to the U.S. Constitution and government selected by the people and for the people. The new party also preeched freedom from federal government intruding on individuals, and states' rights. In the early days, the party shied away from a strong national defense, but the war of 1812 made it very clear for many Democrats that a strong national defense was imperative to our freedoms. In the early 1800's, the party opposed elitism and high taxes, but was split in regard to slavery.

Andrew Jackson won the presidency in 1828. He dropped the Republican part of the party name; he ran and won as a Democrat. It has been known as the Democratic Party since.

In the 1860's (the Civil War era), the Republican Party came to prominence, as they were united against slavery. This issue split apart the Democrats. In the late 1800's, many Democrats, called Bourbon Democrats, fought against corruption and fought for the gold standard to shore up our nations financial status. The Democrats were very conservative in regard to U.S. currency and industry.

The early 1900's marked the Progressive Era (large government income taxes and social liberalism). This socialism actually started with the Republican Party and soon consumed the Democrat party. Under President Woodrow Wilson, America saw massive regulation, elitism, intellectualism, socialism, and progressivism, along with direct income taxes. Wilson stood in vast contrast to everything the Democrat party had once stood for.

The next three presidents were Republicans. Wilson had left the U.S. economy in shambles; we were in a depression with massive unemployment and home values plummeted. President Harding quickly cut spending and taxes by almost 50% each; and within 18 months, America was back on a solid footing of only 2% unemployment. He died of a heart attack, only serving two and a half years into his presidency. Coolidge continued this conservative approach with great results known as "The Roaring Twenties". In the 1930's, Hoover governed during the "Great Depression". He did not really know what to do. As America turned sour on the economic direction of the country, in 1933 Franklin D. Roosevelt was elected and unfortunately continued the progressive, socialist agenda of Wilson. At this time, many Democrats joined with Republicans to stop the socialist carnage of FDR.

In the mid 1900's, many Democrats again started leaning more progressive. (I should say here that the term progressive is just another term for socialist or liberal, and today this term is often used to disguise liberalism and socialism, socialism being big, controlling government). In short order, the party became affiliated with liberal views rather than the conservative platform the party had been known for, for so many years. President Truman continued a socialist agenda, but fortunately conservatives on both sides of the isle joined together in Congress to stop some of his policies. President Eisenhower, a Republican, served the next two terms and also continued a leftist agenda. During this time, organized labor entrenched a foothold on the Democrat party; likewise, the Democrat party entrenched a foothold on organized labor.

John F. Kennedy was elected in 1961, and it was Kennedy that was a spark of sanity for our country. Kennedy worked hard to push back communism, lower taxes, balance the federal budget, stabilize our currency, and re-establish the greatness of America through our space program. President Kennedy was a conservative Democrat, especially with regards to economics. In a later chapter of this book, we will discuss at greater length taxes and the economy. Included at the end of this book is Kennedy's Dec. 14, 1962 speech, most of which covers his program and plans for the economic strength of America.

After Kennedy's assassination, President Johnson followed with a vast array of liberal laws as Congress was divesting itself of conservative values which had held socialism in America to a slow trickle. President Nixon, as you may recall, was a mess. He grew government and destroyed, via scandal, America's confidence in government, especially the Presidency. Ford followed with little confidence from the citizens of America.

President Carter followed Ford with what can only be described, even by many Democrats, as one of the worst presidencies of the Twentieth century. He was the perfect picture of progressivism, and it was not a pretty sight. Under Carter, we had 18% interest rates, 18% inflation, price controls, high unemployment, growing federal deficit, and 70% marginal tax rates, not to mention the Iranian hostage crisis. These conditions brought

America to its knees. The only bright spot that can be shown, in my opinion, is that America saw exactly what progressivism and socialism brings to those who try it.

Ronald Reagan came to the presidency, as the American people had enough of Liberalism run amuck; however, what many people do not realize is that the Democrats helped elect Reagan. Without Democrats in and out of office, his program of drastic tax cuts, regulatory relief, and a strong national defense could not have occurred. It seems that the American people, both Democrats and Republicans, had remembered their roots of freedom; Reagan just led the way. By the way, grass root Democrats followed in big numbers; it worked, and worked in a remarkable way. These "Reagan Democrats," as they were called, lived and voted for the original values of the Democrat party: low taxes, small limited government, and states rights. During these Reagan years, the U. S. enjoyed unprecedented prosperity, growth, and security which lasted far beyond the years of his presidency.

The Reagan conservative policies and the original American conservative beliefs are vastly superior to the new adopted values and policies of socialism. In fact, because of Reagan and Reagan Democrats, socialism, or "Communism," (Communism being one form of Socialism) the former Soviet Union was completely defeated and millions of people were freed from the shackles of poverty, scarcity, and oppression.

In the 1980's, Democrats followed the course of putting party second, and American values and freedom first as they did under President Lincoln in the 1860's. It is a fact that Reagan was a Democrat for many years before he became a Republican. He stated, "*I didn't leave the Democratic Party; It left me.*" On October 27th 1964, in Los Angeles, California, he gave a masterful speech he called "A Time For Choosing." I would like to review some of that speech here, just to give a sample of what we as a nation were facing then, in 1964, and also now, in 2011. Inserted in the back of this book you will find the complete speech; I urge you to read it.

Ronald Reagan

"I have spent most of my life as a Democrat. I recently have seen fit to follow another course. I believe that the issues confronting us cross party lines. Now, one side in this campaign has been telling us that the issues of this election are the maintenance of peace and prosperity. The line has been used, "We've never had it so good."

"But I have an uncomfortable feeling that this prosperity isn't something on which we can base our hopes for the future. No nation in history has ever survived a tax burden that reached a third of its national income. Today, 37 cents out of every dollar earned in this country is the tax collector's share, and yet our government continues to spend 17 million dollars a day more than the government takes in. We haven't balanced our budget 28 out of the last 34 years. We've raised our debt limit three times in the last twelve months, and now our national debt is one and a half times bigger than all the combined debts of all the nations of the world. We have 15 billion dollars in gold in our treasury; we don't own an ounce. Foreign dollar claims are 27.3 billion dollars. And we've just had announced that the dollar of 1939 will now purchase 45 cents in its total value.

"Not too long ago, two friends of mine were talking to a Cuban refugee, a businessman who had escaped from Castro, and in the midst of his story one of my friends turned to the other and said, "We don't know how lucky we are." And the Cuban stopped and said, "How lucky you are? I had someplace to escape to." And in that sentence he told us the entire story. If we lose freedom here, there's no place to escape to. This is the last stand on earth.

"And this idea that government is beholden to the people, that it has no other source of power except the sovereign people, is still the newest and the most unique idea in all the long history of man's relation to man.

"This is the issue of this election: whether we believe in our capacity for self-government or whether we abandon the American revolution and confess that a little intellectual elite in a far-distant capitol can plan our lives for us better than we can plan them ourselves.

"You and I are told increasingly we have to choose between a left or right. Well I'd like to suggest there is no such thing as a left or right. There's only an up or down: [up] man's old – old-aged dream, the ultimate in individual freedom consistent with law and order, or down to the ant heap of totalitarianism. And regardless of their sincerity, their humanitarian motives, those who would trade our freedom for security have embarked on this downward course.

"In this vote-harvesting time, they use terms like the "Great Society," or as we were told a few days ago by the President, we must accept a greater government activity in the affairs of the people. But they've been a little more explicit in the past and among themselves; and all of the things I now will quote have appeared in print.

"These are not Republican accusations. For example, they have voices that say, "The cold war will end through our acceptance of a not undemocratic socialism." Another voice says, "The profit motive has become outmoded. It must be replaced by the incentives of the welfare state." Or, "Our traditional system of individual freedom is incapable of solving the complex problems of the 20th century." Senator Fulbright has said at Stanford University that the Constitution is outmoded. He referred to the President as "our moral teacher and our leader," and he says he is "hobbled in his task by the restrictions of power imposed on him by this antiquated document." He must "be freed," so that he "can do for us" what he knows "is best." And Senator Clark of Pennsylvania, another articulate spokesman, defines liberalism as "meeting the material needs of the masses through the full power of centralized government."

"Well, I, for one, resent it when a representative of the people refers to you and me, the free men and women of this country, as "the masses." This is a term we haven't applied to ourselves in America. But beyond that, "the full power of centralized government" – this was the very thing the Founding Fathers sought to minimize. They knew that governments don't control things. A government can't control the economy without controlling people. And they know when a government sets out to do that, it must use force and coercion to achieve its purpose. They also knew, those Founding Fathers, that outside of its legitimate functions, government does nothing as well or as economically as the private sector of the economy."[1]

Reagan continues explaining the dangers of increasing the size of government, the seizure of private property rights, and other vital issues. I believe this is one of the greatest speeches of the Twentieth century. As mentioned, you can read the entire

---

[1]   A Time For Choosing, by Ronald Reagan, Oct. 1964

text at the end of this book; it is also available to view on Youtube. (A Time for choosing by Ronald Reagan by Reagan foundation)

Reagan was first a Democrat, but he saw the Socialist slide that the Democrats were currently on, and he did not want any part of it. I believe most Democrats today feel the same way Ronald Reagan did in 1964.

The first President George Bush followed Reagan for only one term, as he was not the leader Reagan was, especially with regards to conservative principles; he did not keep his promise of "No New Taxes", and he increased the size of government.

Bill Clinton's presidency saw a sharp return to liberal, or socialist ideals, from the White House, but not from Congress, as the American people reacted to only 21 months of left wing policies such as National health care, weak national defense, and higher taxes. It seems Democrats, and the country for that matter, need to be reminded every so often of the destruction of freedom and prosperity that socialism brings. Mid-term elections gave Republicans a majority in both houses of Congress for the first time in 40 years, and the Republicans did well for a while. Unfortunately, however, they did not persistently lead or did not know how to constantly lead the way toward conservative American principles. Republicans for the most part do follow conservatism, but need to do much better in leading conservatism. The Democrats, on the other hand, seem much more adapt at leading the way, for the good or detriment of our Nation, case in point President Obama; however we will get to his presidency in a bit.

The next George Bush did lead the way much of the time with healthy tax cuts and strong national defense. Unemployment was very low and hopes were high, but he also increased the size of government and spent far more than the American people wanted. We cannot just taste a little conservatism; we need to feast on it. Let me just say here that in my view conservatism is the basic principles of freedom, prosperity, and limited government as set forth in our Constitution, including the traditional American family values as set forth by the American people.

Unfortunately, President Obama and our Democrat Party have abandoned the conservative values which the once great Democrat Party championed. Almost the entire Democrat party has become entrenched in socialism, progressivism, climatism, and corruption. I seek not to let the Republicans off the hook; they also have tentacles testing these evil waters, but they are not leading this destruction: they are simply following, as seems to be their expertise.

The Democrat Party has a passion and a gift to lead. Because of this, it is up to the Democrat party to once again lead this nation into freedom, prosperity, and constitutional values. In doing so, we will also take back our Democrat party and restore it to its glory. I will, in the following chapters, show you how I think the Democrats can and should accomplish this, but first a little evidence of the socialist, progressive train wreck we are headed toward.

CHAPTER 2

SOCIALISM TODAY

President Obama has a background in progressive, socialist thinking. He has said publicly that the Supreme Court did not go as far as they could have to redistribute the wealth of our country. He has also said we need to spread the wealth around. Early Democrats, and our Founding Fathers for that matter, were not interested in spreading the wealth around, but spreading the FREEDOM around. When a government spreads the wealth around, the majority of citizens become poor; when the government spreads the Freedom around, everyone has an equal chance to become prosperous or even wealthy.

Unfortunately for us, President Obama has also surrounded himself with like-minded people who have a very liberal, progressive agenda. John Holdren, Obama's Science Czar, has some very progressive ideas of mass sterilization through drugging our water supply, forced abortions, and population control. He has ideas of a huge planetary regime established to control the world wide economy and a global police force[2]. Ron Bloom, Obama's Manufacturing Czar, has stated that the free market is nonsense and is a joke. He said he agrees with Mao Tse-Tung that power largely comes from the barrel of a gun.[3] Van Jones said, "I met all these young radical people

---

2   Ecoscience by John Holdren, Paul Ehrlich, Ann Ehrlich 1977
3   Ron Bloom speech 2008 Distressed Investors Forum.

of color — I mean really radical, communists and anarchists. And it was, like, 'This is what I need to be a part of.' I spent the next ten years of my life working with a lot of those people I met in jail, trying to be a revolutionary. I was a rowdy nationalist on April 28th. By August, I was a communist."[4] These are the words of Van Jones, the former Green Czar, appointed by President Obama. Another Mao Tse-Tung admirer is Anita Dunn, the President's White House Communications Director. She has stated that Mao is one of her favorite political philosophers.[5] The only problem is that Mao slaughtered over 70 million of his own people.

We also have other elected Democrats who have very similar beliefs and desires for a socialist utopia. Bernie Sanders is a self–described Socialist; Harry Reed and Nancy Pelosi push National Health Care, even against the will of the people. Howard Dean, in April of 2009, speaking to a group of people in Paris, said, "I think the debate for the new generation is instead of Capitalism or Socialism, is are we going to have both , and then which proportion of each should we have".[6] In America should we have both capitalism and socialism? Congressman Spencer Bacchus said 17 members of the U.S. House are socialists.[7] Likewise, some Republicans have lost sight of what makes this county the greatest, freest, most prosperous nation the world has ever seen. It did not happen through socialism, progressivism, or communism; it's actually the opposite of these; it's freedom, capitalism, and the Constitution of the United States of America.

The Congressional Progressive Caucus is one of the largest caucuses in Congress with over 75 members, mostly all Democrats. Their goals are many of the same goals of the Communist Party of America.

---

4   East Bay Express by Eliza Strickland Nov.2, 2005
5   Speech June 5, 2009
6   YouTube, Naked Emperor News1, Howard Dean speech, Paris France 4-5-09
7   Birmingham News April 9, 2009, Politico April 9, 2009

The following list comes right off the Congressional Progressive Caucus website: cpc.grijalva.house.gov/

Caucus Member List

Wednesday January 05, 2011

Co-Chairs

- Keith Ellison Congressman, Minnesota 5th District, Democrat
- Raúl Grijalva, Congressman, Arizona 7th District, Democrat

Vice Chairs

- Tammy Baldwin, Congresswomen, Wisconsin, 2nd District, Democrat
- Judy Chu, Congresswomen, California, 32nd District, Democrat
- William "Lacy" Clay, Congressman, Missouri, 1st District, Democrat
- Sheila Jackson-Lee, Congresswoman, Texas, 18th District, Democrat, Democrat
- Chellie Pingree, Congresswoman, Main, 1st District, Democrat

Senate Members

- Bernie Sanders, U.S. Senator, Vermont, Democrat
- Tom Udall, U.S. Senator, New Mexico, Democrat

House Members

- Xavier Becerra, Congressman, California, 31st District, Democrat
- Earl Blumenauer, Congressman, Oregon, 3rd District, Democrat

- Robert Brady, Congressman, Pennsylvania, 1st District, Democrat.,
- Corrine Brown, Congresswoman, Florida, 3rd District, Democrat
- Michael Capuano, Congressman, Massachusetts, 8th District, Democrat
- Andre Carson, Congressman, Indiana, 7th District, Democrat
- Donna Christensen, Congresswoman, U.S. Virgin Islands, Democrat.
- Yvette Clarke, Congresswoman, New York, 11th District, Democrat
- Emanuel Cleaver, Congressman, Missouri, 5th District, Democrat
- Steve Cohen, Congressman, Tennessee, 9th District, Democrat
- John Conyers, Congressman, Michigan, 14th District, Democrat
- Elijah Cummings, Congressman, Maryland, 7th District Democrat
- Danny Davis, Congressman, Illinois, 7th District, Democrat
- Peter DeFazio, Congressman, Oregon, 4th District, Democrat
- Rosa DeLauro, Congresswoman, Connecticut, 3rd District , Democrat
- Donna Edwards, Congresswoman, Maryland, 4th District, Democrat
- Sam Farr, Congressman, California, 17th District, Democrat
- Chaka Fattah, Congressman, Pennsylvania, 2nd District, Democrat
- Bob Filner, Congressman, California, 51st District, Democrat.
- Barney Frank, Congressman, Massachusetts, 4th District, Democrat.
- Marcia Fudge, Congresswomen, Ohio, 11th District, Democrat
- Luis Gutierrez, Congressman, Illinois, 4th District, Democrat.
- Alcee Hastings, Congressman, Florida, 23rd District, Democrat

- Maurice Hinchey, Congressman, New York, 22nd District., Democrat
- Mazie Hirono, Congresswoman, Hawaii, 2nd District, Democrat
- Michael Honda, Congressman, California, 15th District, Democrat
- Jesse Jackson, Jr., Congressman, Illinois, 2nd District, Democrat.
- Eddie Bernice Johnson, Congresswoman, Texas, 30th District, Democrat.
- Hank Johnson, Congressman, Georgia, 4th District, Democrat.
- Marcy Kaptur, Congresswoman, Ohio, 9th District, Democrat.
- Dennis Kucinich, Congressman, Ohio, 10th District Democrat.
- Barbara Lee, Congresswoman, California, 9th District, Democrat.
- John Lewis, Congressman, Georgia, 5th District, Democrat
- David Loebsack, Congressman, Iowa, 2nd District, Democrat
- Ben Ray Lujan, Congressman, New Mexico, 3rd District, Democrat
- Carolyn Maloney , Congresswoman, New York, 14th District, Democrat.
- Ed Markey, Congressman, Massachusetts, 7th District, Democrat
- Jim McDermott, Congressman, Washington, 7th District, Democrat.
- James McGovern, Congressman, Massachusetts, 3rd District, Democrat.
- George Miller, Congressman, California, 7th District, Democrat.
- Gwen Moore, Congresswoman, Wisconsin, 4th District, Democrat.
- Jim Moran, Congressman, Virginia, 8th District, Democrat
- Jerrold Nadler, Congressman, New York, 8th District, Democrat.
- Eleanor Holmes Norton, Congresswoman, District of Columbia, Democrat.

- John Olver, Congressman, Massachusetts, 1st District, Democrat
- Frank Pallone, Congressman, New Jersey, 6th District, Democrat
- Ed Pastor, Congressman, Arizona, 4th District, Democrat.
- Donald Payne, Congressman, New Jersey, 10th District, Democrat.
- Jared Polis, Congressman, Colorado, 2nd District, Democrat
- Charles Rangel, Congressman, New York, 15th District, Democrat.
- Laura Richardson, Congresswoman, California, 37th District, Democrat.
- Lucille Roybal-Allard, Congresswoman, California, 34th District, Democrat.
- Bobby Rush, Congressman, Illinois, 1st District, Democrat.
- Linda Sanchez, Congresswoman, California, 39th District, Democrat.
- Jan Schakowsky, Congresswoman, Illinois, 9th District, Democrat.
- Jose Serrano, Congressman, New York, 16th District, Democrat.
- Louise Slaughter, Congresswoman, New York, 28th District, Democrat.
- Pete Stark, Congressman, California, 13th District, Democrat.
- Bennie Thompson, Congressman, Mississippi, 2nd District, Democrat.
- John Tierney, Congressman, Massachusetts, 6th District, Democrat.
- Nydia Velazquez, Congresswoman, New York, 12th District, Democrat.
- Maxine Waters, Congresswoman, California, 35th District, Democrat.
- Mel Watt, Congressman, North Carolina, 12th District, Democrat.

- Henry Waxman, Congressman, California, 30th District, Democrat.
- Peter Welch, Congressman, Vermont, Democrat. US
- Lynn Woolsey, Congresswoman, California, 6th District, Democrat.

The Congressional Progressive Caucus website states "Our Caucus members promote a strong progressive agenda". [8]

Again, progressivism is just slang for socialism (Big Government).

It is amazing to me that this Progressive Caucus, or rather this Socialist Caucus, is made up entirely of Democrats, Democrats who have taken a solemn oath before God to protect and defend the Constitution of the United States of America and the freedoms that our Constitution brings. Our Constitution is built to restrict our Federal Government and to keep it small, yet this caucus and the Democrats involved have a goal to socialize our country; as a result, freedoms diminish and government grows.

The following is a report by Snidely Whiplash:

> "Not too awful long ago I wrote about the Communist Party USA and their support for many of the identical principles endorsed by the Democrat Party here in the US. I listed the various similarities but now I have some even more honest words from the Communists themselves. Joe Sims, co-editor of the Communist Party USA online magazine Peoples World states among other things "the possibility that the communists may be able to "capture' the Democratic Party entirely." Read that slowly and carefully..."the possibility that the communists may be able to "capture' the Democratic Party entirely."[9]

---

8   Congressional Progressive Caucus website: About CPC.
9   associatedcontent.com, newzeal.blogspot.com

CHAPTER 3

We Must Vote the Way We Live

WE MUST VOTE THE WAY WE LIVE. I am not sure who first coined this phrase, and I do not even recall when I first heard it; however, for Democrats, and all voters, this is exactly the prescription needed to take back our party and our country. It is horrifying for our party and our country that so many Democrats vote for people who do not hold the same values and beliefs that they, the voters, hold to. *We must vote the way we live.*

I believe there are four main principles on which the <u>current</u> Democrat party rests.

1. Socialism, or BIG GOVERNMENT. The new hip word for Socialism is Progressivism.
2. Redistribution of Wealth, or CLASS WARFARE.
3. Global Warming, RADICAL ENVIRONMENTALISM. I sometimes call it Climatism.
4. Abortion: KILLING BABIES.

In the next few chapters we will discuss these four principles of the current Democrat party in some detail. I think I can show that much of the voting block of our party has much different views, beliefs, values, and standards than those we have elected into office.

We will first start with Socialism (Big Government). This leg or principle of big government is the first, largest, and strongest leg on which the current Democrat party rests. In many ways it controls the scope and size of the other three legs: Redistribution of Wealth, Global Warming, and Abortion. Dictionary.com defines Socialism as:

1. "a theory or system of social organization that advocates the vesting of the ownership and control of the means of production and distribution, of capital, land, etc., in the community as a whole.

Meaning Government as a whole.

(in Marxist theory) the stage following capitalism in the transition of a society to communism, characterized by the imperfect implementation of collectivist principles."[10]

There are many types of Socialism (Communism, Marxism, Fascism, Stalinism, and Democratic Socialism, just to name a few) but all forms of socialism have the same goal of BIG, CONTROLLING GOVERNMENT. Another great definition of Socialism is simply "Too Much Government." When any nation has too much government, three horrible side effects always follow: 1. Oppression, 2. Loss of freedom, and 3. a poor economy. Socialism, or too much government, is far to the left of our political spectrum; on the other hand, far the right is Anarchy, or too little government.

Ronald Reagan gave a speech in 1961. At this time he was a Democrat. He said the following:

"Now back in 1927 an American socialist, Norman Thomas, six times candidate for president on the Socialist Party ticket, said the American people would never vote for socialism. But he said under the name of liberalism, the American people will adopt every fragment of the socialist program."[11]

---

10   Dictionary.com
11   Operation Coffee Cup Campaign against Socialized Medicine,1961. Ronald Reagan

And that is exactly what many Democrats have done, especially those who govern. Our great country will fall apart under socialism, just like any other country will under socialism. Our Founders knew this to be true.

from 1944 to 1964 the Canadian province of Saskatchewan experimented with socialism. W. R Thatcher was elected Premier of Saskatchewan in 1964 after the citizens of this province had enough of this socialist experiment. The following are excerpts from a speech given by Premier Thatcher on November 10, 1966.

"Out of the depths of the depression, the Canadian socialist party was given birth in Saskatchewan. A socialist government was elected in 1944, and an experiment launched, which was unique in Canadian history. I believe that any understanding of Saskatchewan development must include reference to that 20 year chapter. I make no apology for referring to it today.

Let me also make it very clear, that in no way do I question the sincerity of those who participated in the experiment. The overall objectives of the socialists were clear.

(1) Their avowed aim was to "eradicate capitalism". (2) The making of profits was condemned as an unforgivable sin. (3) Government ownership of industry and the means of production, was encouraged and promoted. (4) So called "free social services" were advocated regardless of costs.

How Did the Experiment Succeed?

In 1944, the socialists said they would solve the unemployment problem by building government factories. Not only this, they promised to use the profits from these socialist enterprises to build highways, schools, hospitals, and to finance better social welfare measures generally. Over the years, they set up 22 Crown Corporations.

I wish that time permitted me to tell you of the fiasco which followed. By the time we took over the government 30 months ago, 12 of the Crown Corporations had gone bankrupt or been disposed of. Four more were, in effect, bankrupt-only kept going by government loans and grants. Virtually, without exception, those which had to compete with private enterprise on equal terms, lost huge sums of money regularly and consistently. Even the monopolies, like our Power Corporation, displayed little business efficiency. The experiment cost the taxpayer of Saskatchewan millions of dollars. In 20 years, the socialist experiment in our province certainly demonstrated to any unbiased Canadian that government ownership is no cure-all for economic ailments.

During those two unhappy decades, the socialists waged war against private business. Repeatedly, they demonstrated their hostility, by legislation and actions. Private enterprise became a kind of "dirty word". The results were little short of disastrous. Investors from Eastern Canada, from Europe, from the States, simply turned their back on the socialists they began to avoid Saskatchewan like the plague. During the period when Canada was experiencing the greatest economic boom in her history, Saskatchewan received only a handful of new industries. Oil production, which once reached near-boom proportions in Saskatchewan, dwindled in the late fifties and early sixties. Gas exploration ground almost to a complete stop. Prospecting and mineral exploration in our vast north virtually ceased. Timber production in our north declined drastically.

Unemployment in Saskatchewan during most of the period remained serious. From 1945 to 1963, more than a million new industrial jobs were created across Canada. Yet, in Saskatchewan, after 18 years of socialism, there were fewer jobs in manufacturing than existed in 1945this despite the investment of $500 million in Crown Corporations.

Taxes

As I said earlier, prior to taking office, the socialists had promised a greatly expanded program of social welfare measures. The money to finance these projects was to come from the profits of the crown corporations. Of course, in the overall picture, there were no profits-rather there were colossal losses. Thus, the welfare program had to be financed by huge increases in taxation. During their 20 year administration, 600 completely new taxes were introduced. 650 other levies were increased. "Per capita" taxes in Saskatchewan by 1964 were substantially out of line with the rest of Canada.

Population

In 1945, we had a provincial population which was the third in Canada-we had more people than Alberta, British Columbia, or Manitoba. After 20 years of socialism, Saskatchewan had slipped to sixth place, population-wise, in our Confederation. 270,000 of our citizens left Saskatchewan to find employment elsewhere. Thousands of our university and collegiate graduates were obliged to move out of our province, because there were no jobs at home. In that period, our population growth was the lowest of any province in all Canada.

Socialist Defeat

Finally, 30 months ago, our people decided they had been the Canadian guinea pig for socialism long enough. They threw them out.

Mr. Chairman, is there a lesson to be learned from Saskatchewan's experience with socialism? I think there is a rather horrible lesson. I wish that Canadians in Eastern Canada, who think that socialism is the answer, would come to Saskatchewan, and study what happened to our province in those two decades. 20 years of socialism gave Saskatchewan:

-industrial stagnation, -retarded development, -oppressive taxation, -major depopulation.

We know socialism, not from text books-but from hard, bitter experience. As many of us see it, there is nothing wrong with socialism, except that it won't work.

Private Enterprise Experiment

Since mid-1964, we have reversed our economic method. We inaugurated what we like to call an "experiment in private enterprise", in an effort to obtain new industries and mines. We know, as you do, that the private enterprise system is not perfect. But we also know that under that system, Americans and Canadians have enjoyed the highest living standards in the world.

Our Government recognizes that industrialists will establish in Saskatchewan for only one reason-because it is profitable for them to do so. Accordingly, we are endeavoring to render the political and economic climate safe, desirable and profitable. In the years ahead, we propose to take every feasible step, to make Saskatchewan known as a province where private enterprise is welcomed with "open arms". We intend to keep the burden of taxes and regulation at the lowest possible minimum.

Has this different attitude, has this opposite philosophy, accomplished anything tangible for our people? I believe there have been results-let me give you a few examples.

Timber

One-third of the land in Saskatchewan is covered by timber. In the socialist years, the government maintained a complete monopoly in the production of wood products. Private companies were not only unwelcome, they were prevented by law from locating in our north.

Several years ago we discontinued this monopoly. We sought out lumber and pulp companies from all over the continent, and invited them to invest in Saskatchewan. Moreover, we provided incentives where necessary. The results have been encouraging. Four large lumber complexes have now established in our north, employing from 200 to 300 men each. The most outstanding result has been the establishment of one of the world's largest pulp mills, costing about $65 million. The mill will employ several thousand people in the Prince

Albert Area, in the mill and woods operations. We also are negotiating hopefully for the establishment of a second pulp mill in Saskatchewan."[12]

Clearly capitalism, not socialism, was and is the answer. This is where we need to discuss our Founding Fathers' efforts to find the balanced center of the political arena, where there is **"enough government to keep the peace, but not enough government to oppress the people".**[13] Our Founders largely succeeded in their efforts to find the balanced center. Our Constitution set the United States up as the first free people in modern times. Because of these freedoms, the U.S. surpassed all other nations in technology, prosperity, health, happiness, education, strength, security, etc. all in a very short period of time. At the time of our nation's birth most, if not all, of the other nations should have far exceeded the U.S. in these areas. Yet most of these other countries had, and would continue to have, "Too Much Government" and too few freedoms.

We excelled because our founders placed constraints on our federal government. No other nation had done this. Most, if not all other governments, had complete control and power over the people they governed. America still had laws and government, but just enough to keep the peace and to secure our rights and safety. Our government also had separated powers to further ensure our freedoms. The separation of powers ensured America from excessive power forming in one concentrated place in our government.

Our founders did not find this freedom formula right away; it took some time to experience aspects of government that did not work. Early on in America's history, we actually experimented with Communism. The Plymouth Plantation was one of the first settlements in America; those who came felt that they were

---

12   A New Voice in Confederation, by W. Ross Thatcher. November 10, 1966 speeches. empireclub.org.

13   Dr. W. Cleon Skousen, Miracle of America

there by divine power; they felt they should all live as one under a commune. This experiment with Communism failed; many starved to death. Governor William Bradford finally abandoned communism and gave a parcel of land to each family to own; they were on their own to plant and work according to their desire. This capitalistic venture was very successful; Bradford wrote, "This had very good success; for it made all hands very industrious, so that much more corn was planted than otherwise would have been... The women now went willingly into the fields and took their little ones with them to set corn, which before would allege weakness and inability; whom to have forced would have been thought great tyranny and oppression". (William Bradford, History of Plymouth, pp. 160-162) This little colony now had an abundance of food, so much so that they could trade and share with others.

Shortly after our United States was organized under our constitution, Thomas Jefferson said, "If we can prevent the government from wasting the labors of the people, under the pretense of taking care of them, they must be happy."

Winston Churchill said, "Socialism is a philosophy of failure, the creed of ignorance, and the gospel of envy; its inherent virtue is the equal sharing of misery."

In the 1960's, there was a very interesting individual by the name of Eldridge Cleaver; he was in and out of prison for some years and while in prison became a devout communist. After his release in 1966, he joined one of the new revolutionary groups known as the Black Panthers. With the Black Panthers, tried to burn many of the U.S. cities to the ground. Eldridge Cleaver eventually fled the country and sought refuge in many Communist countries such as Cuba, Red China, Algeria, North Korea, and Russia. He noticed that nowhere was Communism a success; it was just the opposite; Communism was a complete and utter failure everywhere it was tried. Citizens of these Communist countries tried to escape communism. Most tried to flee to America, but no one tried to enter and live in these Communist controlled countries. Eldridge Cleaver eventually came back to America, served his time in prison, and said "I have taken an oath in my heart to oppose communism until the day I die". Dr. W. Cleon Skousen spent some time with Mr. Cleaver and said that "It was clear that he (Eldridge Cleaver) would rather be in prison in America than free in those communist countries". Some time after his parole Eldridge Cleaver took some courses on the history of America and our Founding Fathers. These courses, called "the Miracle of America", were in fact taught by Dr. Skousen. After finishing the Miracle of America course, Eldridge Cleaver said the following, "I wish every family in the United States could hear this great message. If my family had enjoyed these classes when I was growing up, I would have never been a Communist; I would have learned to love America because I would have known her great secrets"[14]. One of the great secrets that Mr. Cleaver was referring to was the principle of Capitalism. Capitalism, unlike Communism, always works.

Our founders worked hard to find the best ways to prosper economically, as stated in Dr. Skousens work "Miracle of America". They found many answers, largely in the writings of Adam Smith. In his work, <u>The Wealth of Nations</u>, he spells out natural laws of economics. Smith advocated prosperity through four main freedoms: 1. Freedom to try. 2. Freedom to buy. 3. Freedom to sell, 4. Freedom to fail. He also advocated specializing in specific areas of manufacturing; for example, having one person making shoes, another making tools, another producing food, yet another sewing clothes, and so on. He advocated all people being free to bring their goods to a common market place to sell them for a profit. Smith determined that when one specializes in a specific good or service, this makes products abundant and cheap. People then prosper because there is a profit attached to the good or service which enables them to make more of the products people want, and also gives them ability to buy other products, supplies or services they need. Adam Smith discovered

---

14   Miracle of America, audio CD

that the wealth of a nation is not necessarily gold or money; it is actually in the abundance of food, clothes, houses, roads, education, transportation, etc.[15]

Dr. Walter Williams reported that in 1790, farmers were 90% of the U.S. labor force. By 1900 only 41% of Americans labored in farms; by 2008 only 3% of us were farmers.[16] That same 3% can not only produce enough food for America, but they can produce almost enough to feed the world. This is true capitalism. If we are free to produce and govern our own lives and business, we can thrive and also bless the lives of others.

Our founders felt that these principles of capitalism, penned by Adams Smith, held the formula for economic success. Nowhere in the world has any country flourished as America under this banner of freedom and capitalism. It is truly a shame that our own Democratic leadership berates capitalism by telling us it is dead and that our problems come from capitalism; it is the opposite which is true. If we return to true capitalism, we will flourish, and so will any one who tries it. Furthermore, our elected officials betray their oath of office when they write and vote for legislation that forces big government programs on the American people and stifles economic competition and capitalism. Take, for example, the 2010 health care bills. Never before in the history of our country has our federal government forced the American people to buy a specific product or item such as health insurance; sadly, Democrats are solely to blame for this horrendous milestone. Not a single Republican voted for Health Care Reform. Over 80% of the American people are satisfied with the quality of their own health care[17], yet our government, led by our own Democratic Party, is trying to kill capitalism.

We as people do not live our lives this way; we love capitalism, we love freedom, we would not force our neighbor to buy the same car or clothes we own. Perhaps we have a small family and

---

15   Miracle of America, Workbook
16   Walter Williams, Untrue Beliefs, Jan. 6, 2010
17   Scott W. Atlas, The Ignored Facts of American Healthcare. Dec. 13, 2010 www.hoover.org

drive a small car; our neighbor, on the other hand, has a large family and needs a larger car. We have no right to force someone to purchase anything. Some people argue that state governments force people to buy auto insurance. This is true, but that is only if you drive a car; we are not forced to drive or buy a car, we can ride a bike, walk, ride the bus, take a taxi, or get rides from a friend. If we choose to purchase a car, most states require the *car* to be properly insured, but we are not forced to buy the car; we have the freedom to choose the car-insurance. In this country we have the RIGHT TO LIFE; we can not be forced to buy health insurance or anything else simply because we live.

If we vote the way we live, we must vote into office those people, regardless of party, who will stand up for capitalism and freedom, not big government. I can only hope more Democrats who believe in capitalism and free markets will run for office.

We must remember that socialism and socialistic principles always bring high prices, scarcity, and a loss of freedom. Freedom and capitalism always bring abundance, low prices, and prosperity.

If we believe and live our lives this way, we should vote this way.

World renowned economist Thomas Sowell, wrote a column on April 20th, 2010 in it he points out the limitations on power and force and what can be accomplished through freedom and knowledge. He writes:

> "Even the totalitarian governments of the 20th century eventually learned the hard way the limits of what could be accomplished by power alone. China still has a totalitarian government today but, after the death of Mao, the Chinese government began to loosen its controls on some parts of the economy, in order to reap the economic benefits of freer markets.[18]

---

18   Thomas Sowell, The Limits of Power, April 20, 2010 Jewishworldreview.com

"As those benefits became clear in higher rates of economic growth and rising standards of living, more government controls were loosened. But, just as market principles were applied to only certain kinds of slavery, so freedom in China has been allowed in economic activities to a far greater extent than in other realms of the country's life, where tight control from the top down remains the norm.

"Ironically, the United States is moving in the direction of the kind of economy that China has been forced to move away from. China once had complete government control of medical care, but eventually gave it up as the disaster that it was.

"The current leadership in Washington operates as if they can just set arbitrary goals, whether "affordable housing" or "universal health care" or anything else — and not concern themselves with the repercussions — since they have the power to simply force individuals, businesses, doctors or anyone else to knuckle under and follow their dictates.

"Friedrich Hayek called this mindset "the road to serfdom." But, even under serfdom and slavery, experience forced those with power to recognize the limits of their power. What this administration — and especially the President — does not have is experience."

"Barack Obama had no experience running even the most modest business, and personally paying the consequences of his mistakes, before becoming President of the United States. He can believe that his heady new power is the answer to all things."[19]

---

19   Thomas Sowell, The Limits of Power, April 20, 2010 Jewishworldreview.com

Next we will address specifically the size of government.

Under our first president, George Washington, our government employed only 350 civilian employees,[20] but there were only 3 million people in the country. Today, there are just over 300 million citizens, so under George Washington's standards, we would need a whopping 35,000 civilian employees. Sounds good, right? It makes sense; we have 100 times the population today than in Washington's time, so we need 100 times more government employees to provide good service to the American people. I think you will be shocked, as I was, to find out the true number of government workers employed by the federal government. It is not 35,000, not 55,000, not even 100,000. It is not 250,000, 500,000, or even 1 Million; we actually have well over 3.5 million government employees, and growing. This is 100 times the ratio of government employees per citizen today than in Washington's day, which is simply not good for us if we are to remain a free and prosperous nation.

The government has grown from 1 government employee serving 8,600 people to 1 government employee serving just 86 people. This is not sustainable; we simply cannot afford this massive size to which our government has grown.

Dennis Cauchon of USA TODAY reports, "The growth in six figure salaries has pushed the average federal worker's pay to $71,206, compared with $40,331 in the private sector". Dramatic raises in salaries for government workers have come in a recession that has lost over 8 million jobs. It also needs to be pointed out that the private sector (lower paying jobs) is taxed to pay the salaries of the federal government workers (higher paying jobs.)

Other reports show that the average salary for federal workers is actually much larger than Couchon's numbers– more like $120K per year.

---

20   www. nccs.net

Sam Webb (Leader of the Communist Party USA) gave a speech shortly after President Obama was elected. He said, "The U.S. is now on the road to Socialism."[21] Actually, the massive size of our federal government shows that we have been on this road to Socialism for some time; at some time, we will need to get off. Every sector of our economy is currently shrinking except our federal government. If this continues, we will lose more and more of our freedoms and income. It is up to us Democrats to make the necessary changes to downsize our government. The government serves us, the American people; we do not serve the government.

Large government not only taxes the people out of prosperity, but it regulates business out of success. In America, we now have the highest corporate taxes in the industrial world. At the same time, we have heaped massive regulations upon business. Companies no longer seek to locate and grow their business in the U.S. It's no wonder unemployment is skyrocketing.

When speaking of big government, we must also speak of the gross inefficiency of big Socialist government. A Stephen Ohlemacher report shows that "89,000 stimulus payments went to people who were either dead or in prison, around 18 million dollars of waste",[22] and that is just a drop in the bucket. This is what big government does best, waste our hard earned money. Billions and billions have been spent on ridiculous and wasteful projects. In a story by Jeffrey Anderson the jobs provided by the stimulus cost the American taxpayer $278,000 per job. Here is a portion of that report.

> The report was written by the White House's Council of Economic Advisors, a group of three economists who were all handpicked by Obama, and it chronicles the alleged success of the "stimulus" in adding or saving jobs. The council reports that, using "mainstream estimates of econom-

---

21 Aaron Klein, World Net Daily, Dec. 1,2008
22 Stephen Ohlemacher, Associated Press, Oct. 7, 2010

ic multipliers for the effects of fiscal stimulus" (which it describes as a "natural way to estimate the effects of" the legislation), the "stimulus" has added or saved just under 2.4 million jobs — whether private or public — at a cost (to date) of $666 billion. That's a cost to taxpayers of $278,000 per job.

In other words, the government could simply have cut a $100,000 check to everyone whose employment was allegedly made possible by the "stimulus," and taxpayers would have come out $427 billion ahead.

Furthermore, the council reports that, as of two quarters ago, the "stimulus" had added or saved just under 2.7 million jobs — or 288,000 more than it has now. In other words, over the past six months, the economy would have added or saved more jobs *without* the "stimulus" than it has with it. In comparison to how things would otherwise have been, the "stimulus" has been working in reverse over the past six months, causing the economy to shed jobs.[23]

Citizens Against Government Waste is a nonpartisan, nonprofit organization dedicated to eliminating waste, fraud, and abuse, in our government. They report that in 2009 our government spent $3.8 million for the Old Tiger Stadium Conservancy in Detroit; additional examples of this waste include:

$1.9 million for the Pleasure Beach water taxi service in Connecticut;

$1.8 million for swine odor and manure management research in Ames, Iowa;

---

23   Obama's Economists: Stimulus has cost $278,000 per job, Jeffery Anderson, July 3, 2011, Weekly Standard. com

$380,000 for a recreation and fairgrounds area in Kotzebue, Alaska;

$143,000 for the Greater New Haven Labor History Association in Connecticut;

$95,000 for the Canton Symphony Orchestra Association in Ohio; and

$71,000 for Dance Theater Etcetera in Brooklyn for its Tolerance through Arts initiative, just to name a few.[24]

On the other hand, small government is always more efficient, less wasteful, and more accountable. This fact is why our founders wanted states to govern themselves and the Federal Government to be very limited in its powers. Limited powers for federal government was a completely new idea, but our founders knew this would keep government small and efficient and our freedoms safe.

The best current examples of Socialism and big government are Greece, Portugal, Spain, and to some extent, the rest of Europe. Years of extremely high taxes and entitlements have brought these governments to their knees. They now seek bailouts from other countries. Rioting from citizens shows just how difficult it is to make a U-turn from socialism, the socialism which never works, the result of which is always the same: scarcity, poverty, and loss of freedoms.

The following is a portion of an article by Mona Charen,

"One in three Greeks works for the government. Government employees enjoy higher wages, more munificent benefits, and earlier retirements than private sector employees. Civil servants can retire after 35 years of service at 80 percent of their highest salary and enjoy lavish health plans, vacations, and other perks. Because they are so numerous, and because Greece is highly centralized, public sector unions hardly have to negotiate.

---

24   www.cagw.org/reports/pig-book/2009/

They simply vote in their preferred bosses. Some civil servants receive bonuses for using computers, others for arriving at work on time. Forestry workers get a bonus for outdoor work. All civil servants receive 14 yearly checks for 12 months' work. And it's impossible to fire them – even for the grossest incompetence. By the end of 2011, Greece's debt will be 150 percent of its GDP"[25]

No wonder Greece is failing; socialism always fails.

I recently saw a video of prominent Democrat Leader Al Sharpton saying the following "The dream is to make everything equal in everybody's house."[26] That might be a good dream if you want everyone to be prosperous, but socialism always brings equal poverty and misery, not prosperity. We cannot force prosperity, but usually socialism forces all to poverty; case in point: Communist Russia, Communist China, Cuba, Venezuela, and a host of others. Venezuela used to be the most prosperous and wealthy nation south of the U.S. border. Now, with a Socialist dictator in charge, they have forced black outs every night because there is no money to keep the electricity going. Their food is rationed; the poor are poorer and the wealthy are no longer wealthy. Everyone who can get out has; many others are trying.

---

25   Mona Charen, "Athens or Washington, It's the Size of Government" Patriot Post, May 7, 2010
26   video posted on Gateway Pundit by Jim Hoft, May 5th 2010

CHAPTER 4

NATIONAL DEBT

When George Washington became our first president, our national debt was over $75 million, mostly because of the Revolutionary War. President Washington and the succeeding presidents were very serious about paying down the debt. Within a few years, they succeeded, raising money by import duties, a tax on whiskey, and selling land. There were no income taxes and hardly any sales taxes. By 1836, the U.S. Government had not only gotten completely out of debt, but had running surpluses, which they gave back to the states. From time to time, it was necessary to go into debt because of war, but at the war's end we quickly began paying off the debt.

In stark contrast, our national debt today is over $14 Trillion. Our debt increases $100,000 every 10 seconds, which is $10,000 every second. The debt per citizen is well over $40,000 or $118,000 per household, and increasing. We must stop this madness, or it will stop us. We could not live our personal lives this way; we can do better. Our national debt is greater than all other nations' debt combined. Our taxes go up and up; the government gets bigger and bigger, and states no longer enjoy states' rights.

Thomas Jefferson, the founder of the Democratic Party, said, "We shall all consider ourselves unauthorized to saddle posterity with our debt, and morally bound to pay them ourselves, and consequently within what may be deemed the period of a generation or life of the majority".

John Adams said, "There are two ways to enslave a nation. One is by the sword. The other is by debt"

George Washington said, "As a very important source of strength and security, cherish public credit. One method of preserving it is to use it as sparingly as possible… avoiding like-wise the accumulation of debt, not only of shunning occasions of expense, but by vigorous exertion in time of peace to dis-charge the debt witch unavoidable wars may have occasioned."

The following includes excerpts from testimony given on Feb. 3rd, 2011 by Chris Edwards before the Committee on the Budget, United States Senate.

> "Given that American governments already consume more than 40 percent of the nation's GDP, it is extremely unlikely that the government could find new projects with sufficiently high re-turns to make them worthwhile."
>
> Policymakers should reject the idea that added spending is good and beneficial for the econo-my. It isn't. In recent decades, the federal gov-ernment has expanded into hundreds of areas that would be better left to state and local gov-ernments, businesses, charities, and individuals. That expansion is sucking the life out of the pri-vate economy and creating a top-down bureau-cratic society. Cutting federal spending would also enhance personal freedoms by dispersing power from Washington. Historically, America's robust economic growth and high living standards were built on our relatively smaller government than Europe and elsewhere. But if we continue down the current high-spending path, we will become just another sluggish welfare state. Projections by the Congressional Budget Office under its "alter-native fiscal scenario," show that federal spending

will climb by another 11 percentage points of GDP by 2035 unless we make major reforms. Such a spending expansion would doom young people to unbearable levels of taxation and an economy with few opportunities and little innovation.

We need major federal spending cuts. We should cut entitlements, domestic spending, and defense." "Some economists argue that spending cuts would hurt the economy. But consider a real-world experiment of substantial budget-cutting — the Canadian reforms of the 1990s. In the early 1990s, overspending had pushed the size of the Canadian government to 53 percent of GDP, and government debt was soaring. The center-left Liberal government then reversed course and began cutting spending in 1995. Over two years, they chopped 10 percent from total federal spending — equivalent to Congress cutting spending about $370 billion in two years. Then the government held spending at roughly the lower level for another three years.

"As spending was cut, the Canadian economy did not stagnate — it boomed. Indeed, it boomed for the next 15 years until it was hit by the recent U.S.-caused recession. Canadian government spending has fallen by more than 10 percentage points of GDP and the federal budget was balanced 10 years in a row. At the same time, the government spurred growth with pro-market reforms such as free trade, corporate tax cuts, and privatization. The Canadian model of sharp spending cuts and microeconomic reforms to boost growth is an excellent model for U.S. policymakers to follow."[27]

27   Chris Edwards, Challenges to the U.S. Economic Recovery: Federal and State Spending, cato.org Feb. 3rd 2011

In the summer of 2011, the big debate in Congress and the White House was over raising the National Debt Limit. The National Debt approaches 15 Trillion dollars, and we want to raise the debt even more. This is precisely why we have a debt limit; it is there to insure we do not go over that limit. President Barack Obama has spent more in the first three years of his presidency than any other president in history. Yet' he fights for more spending, hoping that he can tax us even more to pay for his recklessness. This is right out of the progressive, socialist playbook: spend more, tax more, grow government more. At some point there just isn't any more.

In July 2011 the U.S. House of Representatives passed a bill known as Cut, Cap, and Balance, that would raise the debt limit but seek spending cuts and a Balanced Budget Amendment. Even four Democrats voted for the bill, but the Democrats lead by Harry Reid in the Senate voted the bill down. Harry Reid said that the bill was "some of the worst legislation in the history of this country."[28]

I can hardly believe that our Democratic leader in the Senate actually thinks that cutting spending and balancing the national budget is bad for our country.

I strongly believe most Americans, Democrats included, would not saddle their children with debt that would be almost impossible for them to pay back. We would not, and do not, purchase a $5 million home and demand our children sign the bank loan, knowing that we are not able to pay it ourselves. Yet' we continually vote for people that place us in such a mess. I will say this many times throughout the pages of this work, and I will say it here, *WE MUST VOTE THE WAY WE LIVE.*

In vast contrast to our federal government, some states in America are getting their financial house in order. In fact, Ben Wolfgang of The Washington Times, reports "Many States celebrate surpluses as Congress struggles with debt". He writes,

---

28   Elise Foley, Huffington Post. 7-21-11

"Unlike Washington, nearly all states are required by law to balance their budgets each year."[29]

Most, if not all, of these states with revenue surpluses have Republican governors who have lowered taxes, and cut spending; as a result, they have rainy day funds, extra money for education, and bonuses for government employees. If we are honest with ourselves we must realize that this is the right way to go. Democrats must get back to this same pattern of responsibility.

---

29   Ben Wolfgang, The Washington Post, July 18, 2011

CHAPTER 5

NATIONAL HEALTH CARE

The Democratic Party has been so infiltrated with Socialism that Democrat leaders in the White House and in Congress have passed into law a national health care system which the American people, by overwhelming numbers, do not want any part of. A discussion and study on big government would not be complete without looking at this socialistic tactic of national health care.

In 1961, Ronald Reagan gave a masterful speech against socialized medicine. He was adamantly opposed to anything that would move us closer to socialized medicine. He tried to educate the American people about bills that would bring socialized medicine to our country. One can actually listen to his speech on YouTube under "Ronald Reagan Speaks Out Against Socialized Medicine".

At the time of this speech, Reagan was not a Republican; he was a Democrat, a Democrat who fought for freedom and limited government.

Eighty percent of the American people are satisfied or very satisfied with the health care they receive here in the U.S.[30] This is no surprise; we have the greatest health care in the world. It is expensive, but we get what we pay for. In the early 1990's, the Clintons pushed hard for a national health care system, and the people flatly rejected it. Many countries have tried this approach, and it has never worked even close to the excellent levels of care we have in the U.S. In most cases, it fails with catastrophic

---

30   Gallup poll Sept. 23, 2009. Gallup.com

consequences. Most countries with national health care are barely on life support, and every country trying this approach finds the same results: much higher costs and much lower coverage and care.

Shockingly, even four of our own states have tried socialized medicine: Maine, Tennessee, Massachusetts, and Hawaii. In all four cases, it has failed, and failed miserably. California tried in 2008 to enact a socialized health plan, but after the true costs and shortfalls were revealed, they could not secure the votes to pass it.

Tennessee's Tenncare started in 1994 and it is now a huge problem. Its costs have skyrocketed; in 2005, they dumped 170,000 people from the plan. The huge cost of Tenncare even threatened to bankrupt the state. Tenncare also caused private health care costs to rise sharply. TennCare was planned to prove that the Clinton national health care program would work; it was the Clinton pattern that Tennessee used to set up the program. However, they are having a hard time even getting doctors to enter the program because the doctors currently providing care within the program are having a hard time getting paid. Usually, only 40% of the costs of services are rendered, if at all, even though Medicaid pays around 50%. Doctors are simply opting out; as a result, health care becomes less available in Tennessee.[31]

Massachusetts' universal health care was enacted in 2006 under Republican Mitt Romney. This plan was established to provide health insurance for the poor and to force others not currently insured to buy health insurance. Massachusetts is facing massive deficits and the highest insurance premiums in the nation. The state is currently trying to remove people from the rolls as fast as possible, and even doctors who once supported the universal health care plan have said that it has failed to reduce medical spending. It is also taking crucial funds from other resources, like

---

31   Lessons from health care reform, July 22, 2009 by Marsha Blackburn and Phil Rose, Real Clear Politics

Emergency Room care. Massachusetts requires every resident to have health insurance; their once bare-bones policies are no longer accepted by the state. The people are forced to get the kind of insurance the state demands, the kind that is very pricey and covers things a citizen may not even need or want. Of course, if one does not get what the state demands, he or she pays a hefty fine. Romney, who thought universal health care could be achieved in his state, has recently declared that the plan does have big problems.

The problems with socialized medicine in Massachusetts are so bad that Massachusetts citizens elected Republican Scott Brown to the Kennedy Senate seat. The Massachusetts citizens have a unique perspective on universal health care, and they do not wish our country as a whole to follow this pattern. Scott Brown pledged to vote against President Obama's socialized health care program, and many Democrats voted the way they lived and placed him in office. This same negative feeling over National Health care has swept the entire nation; yet' the Democrat party continues to push this disastrous program at its own peril, going against the will of the people, making secret deals behind closed doors, and providing payoffs to selected states to get elected officials on board. This activity is the very definition of corruption. The average Democrat does not live his or her life this way; we can do better.

In 2004, Maine started its health care reform public option. Maine's plan was to have so many people enrolled that it could keep costs and premiums down. The fact is that only about 3,000 to 4,000 people have been enrolled as of May 2009, at a cost of $300 million. This disaster has cost the taxpayer of Maine over $90,000 per enrollee. The average private insurance coverage is only $6,000 per year. So many people are now leaving the system that the number of uninsured citizens remains the same as it was before program started (10%) in addition premiums for the health care system have shot up by 70% while premiums for self-employed families cost over $1,500 per month; however, one can purchase excellent health care plan from a private insurer for $300 to $700 per month.[32]

When the government gets involved where only the private market should, costs are always highly inflated, quality goes down, and products become scarce.

Last, but not least, we need to discuss Hawaii's great universal health care plan. As the previous three plans, its main goal was to insure the uninsured. It, too, was a complete failure. It lasted for a whole seven months before it went broke and was terminated. It is human nature to want something cheaper, and the citizens of Hawaii left their expensive private programs to enter the public program. The system, however, could not handle it, so seven months after it started, the governor pulled the plug.

Many people refer to Canada as an example of successful national health care. I received this e-mail some years ago, and I thought it would give some light on the Canadian system.

Canada's Health care system from a Canadian's point of view:

Hey Guys; I've seen on the news up here in Canada how Hillary Clinton introduced her new health care plan, something similar to what we have in Canada. I also heard that Michael Moore was raving about the health care up here in Canada in his latest movie. As your friend, and someone who lives with the Canada health care plan, I thought I would give you some facts about this great medical plan that we have in Canada.

First of all:

1) The health care plan in Canada is not free. We pay a premium every month of $96 for Shirley and I to be covered. Sounds great, eh. What they don't

32   In Main, good intentions paved the road to health-care hell, by David Freddoso, washingtonexaminar.com

tell you is how much we pay in taxes to keep the health care system afloat. I am personally in the 55% tax bracket. Yes, 55% of my earnings go to taxes. A large portion of that, and I am not sure of the exact amount, goes directly to health care, our #1 expense.

2) I would not classify what we have as health care plan; it is more like a health diagnosis system. You can get into to see a doctor quickly enough so he can tell you "yes indeed, you are sick," or, "you need an operation," but now the challenge becomes getting treated or operated on. We have waiting lists out the ying yang, some as much as 2 years down the road.

3) Rather than fix what is wrong with you, the usual tactic in Canada is to prescribe drugs. "Have a pain? Here is a drug to take"- not "What is causing the pain and why?" No time for checking you out because it is more important to move as many patients thru as possible each hour for Government re-imbursement

4) Many Canadians do not have a family Doctor.

5) Don't require emergency treatment as you may wait for hours in the emergency room waiting for treatment.

6) Shirley's dad cut his hand on a power saw a few weeks back and it required that his hand be put in a splint - to our surprise we had to pay $125 for a splint because it is not covered under health care, plus, we have to pay $60 for each visit for him to check it out each week.

7) Shirley's cousin was diagnosed with a heart blockage. Put on a waiting list . Died before he could get treatment.

8) Government allots so many operations per year. When that is done, no more operations, unless you go to your local newspaper and plead your case and embarrass the government; then money suddenly appears.

9) The Government takes great pride in telling us how much they are increasing the funding for health care, but waiting lists never get shorter. Government just keeps throwing money at the problem, but it never goes away. But they are good at finding new ways to tax us, but they don't call it a tax anymore; it is now a "user fee."

10) My mother needs an operation for a blockage in her leg but because she is a smoker they will not do it, despite she and my father paying into the health care system all these years. My Mom is 80 years of age. Now there is talk that maybe we should not treat fat and obese people either because they are a drain on the health care system. Let me see now, what we want in Canada is a health care system for healthy people only. That should reduce our health care costs.

11) Forget getting a second opinion, what you see is what you get.

12) I can spend what money I have left after taxes on booze, cigarettes, junk food, and anything else that could kill me but I am not allowed by law to

spend my money on getting an operation I need because that would be jumping the queue. I must wait my turn, except if I am a hockey player or athlete; then I can get looked at right away. Go figger. Where else in the world can you spend money to kill yourself, but not allowed to spend money to get healthy?

13) Oh, did I mention that immigrants are covered automatically at tax payer expense, having never contributed a dollar to the system and pay no premiums.

14) Oh yeah we now give free needles to drug users to try and keep them healthy. Wouldn't want a sickly druggie breaking into your house and stealing your things. But people with diabetes who pay into the health care system have to pay for their needles because it is not covered but the health care system.

I send this out not looking for sympathy but as the election looms in the states, you will be hearing more and more about universal health care down there, and the advocates will be pointing to Canada. I just want to make sure that you hear the truth about health care up here and have some food for thought and informed questions to ask when broached with this subject.

Step wisely and don't make the same mistakes we have.

I don't even know this person, but I do have friends from Canada that say basically the same thing: very high taxes, easy to see a doctor but long, long, lines to get any procedure done. One of Canada's own, Danny Williams, the Premier of Canada's east coast province recently went to the US for heart surgery because it was not available to him in his province. Is this what we want in the U.S.? I don't, and I am confident most citezens don't either. The polls show that 80% of the American people do not want any part of socialized health care, yet our president and most of the Democratic Party think they know what is good for us, so they are trying any means they can, even unethical means, such as changing procedures in the Congress, to pass the bill without even voting for it. President Obama, on several occasions, declared reconciliation a non-option to pass such legislation, yet now he declares it a viable option. We need Democrats who stand up to the Democratic leadership of Harry Reid and Nancy Pelosi and vote the way the people want.

Now, our health care system is by no means perfect, but it is the best in the world. Most of the new health care innovation is discovered and developed in the U.S. We fund it because we have the money. We then export our innovations to other countries who have no money to fund health care research and development because their socialist systems of health care has no funding for research.

Can the U.S. health care system be improved? Yes, it can, but we can do it through freedom and capitalism (being able to buy insurance across state lines, health care savings accounts, bundling groups, tort reform, less regulation, less government intrusion), not socialism. In other words we just set the American people free to fix our problems, and they, as always will come through.

CHAPTER 6

EDUCATION

Education in America also plays a big role in our massive government. Our public school system is a mess. Even though we pay more per student than any other nation, our students are failing. Our own Education and Labor Committee says that we have a High School Dropout Crisis. Nationally, only 70% of all students in the U.S. graduate from high school, and many who do graduate still have problems with reading, writing, and math. According to Pro Literacy Worldwide, American business spend over $60 billion each year on employee training, with much of that spent on teaching their employees remedial reading, writing and math. The Alliance for Excellent Education has found that only 31% of 8th graders meet the National Assessment of Educational Progress standards of reading proficiency, and the same is true for students in 12th grade. Among low-income 8th graders, only 15% are reading at a proficient level. This, of course, means 85% of those 8th graders are lacking in their reading skills. [33]

On January 26th 2011, the big news story of the day was about an Ohio mom who was sent to jail for sending her two kids to a better public school that was outside of her school district.[34]

Many studies have shown that in the U.S., we spend more per student than any other country. Although we spend $10,000-$12,000 per student on average, our kids get consistently lower test scores in math, science and reading than other nations,

---

33   information compiled by International Reading Association
34   newsfeed.time.com/2011/01/26

nations that spend far less per student. Kids in the U.S. never even score in the top ten anymore and often do not score in the top 20 nations. For example, Korea spends around $4,000 per year per student, and they consistently rank much higher than the U.S. kids in math and science. Korea is not alone; other countries like Singapore, Hong Kong, Japan, Belgium, Hungary, Czech Republic, and many others also spend less, yet score higher in math, science, and reading.

One of the biggest stories in 2011 was the public school cheating scandal in Atlanta Georgia. 82 teachers admitted to changing students' tests, even erasing students' answers and replacing them with the correct answer. This was happening for 10 years, with 140 teacher and 38 principals who were implicated in actually helping students cheat on state tests.[35]

On the other side of the coin, we have the private school system in America. Kids in private schools in the U.S. score consistently higher in math, science, geography, reading and writing than kids in public schools. There is one area that private schools score much lower, and that is in the cost per student. Yes, lower; on average it costs only $7,000 per year, per student to attend a private school.

I would like to take time here to comment on my own experience in both public and private schools. I attended many private and public schools as my mom strived to give my siblings and me a good education. Out of the four private schools I attended, I believe only one pushed me hard academically and provided a great superior education. Of course, it was hard. I was not a great student, so I pushed to attend my local public school to take things a little easier, and that is exactly what I did. Also I must add that my kids do attend our local public school, and they are receiving a great education. In the public school system, there are schools which do achieve high standards of learning, and there are also many schools which have a very low standard and pass the students just to get them out of the system. This is

---

35   US News.com by Jason Koebler, July 7th 2011

where school choice or a voucher system is so important, yet who stands in the way? Yes, it is the Democrats who consistently block our citizens from sending their kids to better schools that often cost less.

According to a recent Newsweek poll "66% of blacks in the U.S., and 67% of Hispanics support a voucher system"[36] where they can choose a specific private school or public school to educate their kids, however, most of the Democrats in the Congress and our current democratic president oppose a voucher system, even though they send their kids to private schools. This is pure hypocrisy. Even worse than this, most of the minority citizens that want school choice keep voting for Democrats that don't want school choice. Again, we must vote the way we live; if we want school choice, than we must vote for Democrats, (or for that matter, Republicans), who vow to vote for school choice. Some areas of the country have over 90% approval among minority groups for a voucher system, yet the elected officials in their own party continue to deny them this important opportunity.

Our own President Obama signed a spending bill into law in March of 2009 that ended, (Yes, I said ENDED) a very popular and successful voucher program that gave low income families $7,500.00 a year to send their children to private schools in Washington DC.[37] Even President Obama's kids go to one of the private schools that participated in this voucher system, but no more; now it's only for the elite. In February of 2008, then presidential candidate Obama said he was open to a voucher program, but then in June of 2008 declared he was not for a voucher system. In 2009 he killed it. Studies show that black students who attend private schools through voucher programs do better in math and reading tests. What are we doing? If we want our children to have the best education possible, we must vote the way we live.

The U.S. Department of Education has over 5,000 employees and 29 different official departments; it has an annual budget

36   The New York Times, by Juan Williams, June 16, 2004
37   Bloomberg.com, by Molly Peterson, April 15, 2009

of over $67 billion, not including $100 billion in additional funding from the American Recovery and Reinvestment Act of 2009. All this money is just for a federal agency (Department of Education). It does not include any state spending on education, which, by the way, is the majority of educational spending in America. Yet what do we hear from our government when asked about the dismal results of our students? They say we need to spend more money; code words for: we need the American people to pay more taxes. Yet, the more we pay the worse things get. If more money was the answer than our kids would have the best test scores in the world every year and in every subject, but as stated earlier they hardly score in the top twenty.

CHAPTER 7

ENERGY

We have elected Democrats who constantly say that America needs to cut its dependency on foreign oil, and then these same elected officials turn right around, regulate and legislate against any possibility of obtaining more of our own domestic energy resources. Our government, largely through the Democratic leadership, has virtually made it impossible to explore and cultivate our own offshore or onshore oil. China is currently exploring 60 miles off the Florida Coast, and Cuba has granted leases for a number of other countries to explore for oil.[38] The U.S could and should be doing the same, and we would not have to go through Cuba to do so; it's right off our own coast. But we don't. We used to be the largest exporter of oil and energy; now we are the largest importer.

Canada, South America, Russia, China, the Middle East, and a host of other countries do everything in their power to obtain their own oil, but we cannot. We have the best technology to explore and drill, and to do so in a cleaner and safer manner than anyone,- yet we don't do it. Between ANWR, Bakken, and offshore oil reserves, we have over 400 billion barrels of oil right in our own backyard; this is enough to keep America supplied with oil for over 50 years without getting oil from any other countries.

According to the Bureau of Land Management and the U.S. Department of the Interior, we have another 800 billion barrels

---

38   www.factcheck.org by Emi Kolawole

of recoverable oil in oil shale in Utah, Colorado, and Wyoming.[39] In addition to this asset, we have over 1,747 trillion cubic feet of natural gas offshore in the U.S. If we used natural gas for all of our energy needs, this source would still keep us going for 150 years or more.

The United States used to be the largest producer of oil. We cannot continue to preach independence from foreign oil and at the same time obstruct the American people from exploring and cultivating our own vast resources of oil, coal, natural gas, and nuclear power. Our government, through the Department of Energy, the EPA, and Congressional Legislation, has regulated the U.S. into the worst energy problem we have had in the last 30 years. Individual states should have the right, (under the constitution they do have the right), to cultivate energy from their own resources as they see fit.

We import more oil from Canada than anywhere else, yet we have more oil in the U.S. than they do. Our own party continually places road blocks in the path of using it. We have more oil and energy resources available right in our own country than we could possibly use in 150 years. Energy exploration and production used to be a large source of income and jobs for the American people. It can, and must be again.

In 2010 and 2011, unemployment has been around 10%. If we count the frustrated unemployed no longer seeking jobless benefits, the unemployment rate is over 17%. Unemployment among Black Americans is also around 17%. If Democrats really want to put people back to work, we must vote for those individuals who will let us be truly energy independent, those who will lift drilling and exploring bans and lift regulations, and legislation currently in place. We can build domestic energy that will undoubtedly put hundreds of thousands of Americans back to work with high paying jobs; at the same time we can lower our energy costs. This could be done on a national level, as well as a state

---

39   http://ostsies.anl.gov/guide/oilshale/

level. California has the worst economic situation it has ever had. It is bankrupt. However, California also has vast energy in off shore oil that, if acquired, could be a great help to California's situation. 51% of California citizens back off-shore drilling,[40] yet the state government refuses to proceed. This situation is what occurs when governments get too large; freedoms are lost, and prosperity stops.

Some say we need clean alternative energy solutions that do not harm our environment. Our environmental policy as a party and a nation will be discussed in the next chapter, but we should cover the economic possibility of alternative sources of energy. We are making some strides in solar, wind, hydrogen, and a few other promising alternative energy sources; but the fact is, as of now these sources are very inefficient and costly. All together they meet only 7% of our current needs. I have no doubt that in the future these alternative sources of energy will improve and will be welcomed. Naturally, CAPITALISM and FREEDOM will be the key to succeed in cultivating alternative sources of energy. Set the American people free, get the government out of our way, and we will find the answers, the answers that are ABUNDANT AND INEXPENSIVE.

Of the 7% of the energy from alternative sources 34% is hydropower, 53% is biomass (Plant materials and animal waste), 1% is solar, and 7% is wind.[41] We have been doing well with hydropower and biomass, but wind and solar have so far proven to be very inefficient and costly. However our government continues to waste our money, trying to force something that is clearly not working. Billionaire T. Boon Pickens had plans to build the largest wind farm in America, but quickly backed off his plans as the cost of wind versus the small return of energy was too much to take. Other sources are cheaper, work better, and can be obtained more easily.

---

40   http://articles.sfgate.com, by Jane Kay, July 31, 2008
41   http://tonto.eia.doe.gov/ , Energy in Brief, April 22, 2009

Some say that we then must conserve energy by simply using less; we should suffer a little for the good of the nation. This will not, however, bring anything good to any one. It will bring fewer freedoms, fewer jobs, less prosperity, and even higher costs.

Ross Mckitrick: Professor of Economics at the University of Guelph, in Ontario Canada, wrote the following.

Earth Hour: A Dissent

Ross McKitrick

In 2009 I was asked by a journalist for my thoughts on the importance of Earth Hour. Here is my response.

> I abhor Earth Hour. Abundant, cheap electricity has been the greatest source of human liberation in the 20th century. Every material social advance in the 20th century depended on the proliferation of inexpensive and reliable electricity. Giving women the freedom to work outside the home depended on the availability of electrical appliances that free up time from domestic chores. Getting children out of menial labor and into schools depended on the same thing, as well as the ability to provide safe indoor lighting for reading.

> Development and provision of modern health care without electricity is absolutely impossible. The expansion of our food supply, and the promotion of hygiene and nutrition, depended on being able to irrigate fields, cook and refrigerate foods, and have a steady indoor supply of hot water. Many of the world's poor suffer brutal environmental conditions in their own homes because of the necessity of cooking over indoor fires that burn twigs and dung. This causes local deforestation and the proliferation of smoke- and parasite-related lung diseases. Anyone who wants to see local conditions improve in the third world should realize the

importance of access to cheap electricity from fossil-fuel based power generating stations. After all, that's how the west developed.

The whole mentality around Earth Hour demonizes electricity. I cannot do that, instead I celebrate it and all that it has provided for humanity. Earth Hour celebrates ignorance, poverty and backwardness. By repudiating the greatest engine of liberation it becomes an hour devoted to anti-humanism. It encourages the sanctimonious gesture of turning off trivial appliances for a trivial amount of time, in deference to some ill-defined abstraction called "the Earth," all the while hypocritically retaining the real benefits of continuous, reliable electricity. People who see virtue in doing without electricity should shut off their fridge, stove, microwave, computer, water heater, lights, TV and all other appliances for a month, not an hour. And pop down to the cardiac unit at the hospital and shut the power off there too.

I don't want to go back to nature. Travel to a zone hit by earthquakes, floods and hurricanes to see what it's like to go back to nature. For humans, living in "nature" meant a short life span marked by violence, disease and ignorance. People who work for the end of poverty and relief from disease are fighting against nature. I hope they leave their lights on.

Here in Ontario, through the use of pollution control technology and advanced engineering, our air quality has dramatically improved since the 1960s, despite the expansion of industry and the power supply. If, after all this, we are going to take the view that the remaining air emissions outweigh all the benefits of electricity, and that we

ought to be shamed into sitting in darkness for an hour, like naughty children who have been caught doing something bad, then we are setting up unspoiled nature as an absolute, transcendent ideal that obliterates all other ethical and humane obligations. No thanks. I like visiting nature but I don't want to live there, and I refuse to accept the idea that civilization with all its tradeoffs is something to be ashamed of.
Ross McKitrick
Professor of Economics
University of Guelph

Currently, we do export a little oil, however, if we were to be set free we would produce most, if not all, of our oil and energy needs, and export even more to other countries resulting in income directly to the American people; it will lower our energy costs in the U.S. and put people to work. It is lunacy for our government and president to publicly announce the goal of reducing our dependency on foreign oil and then block efforts to drill for our own oil.

Harold Hamm, CEO of Continental Resources, believes we can become completely independent of OPEC and provide all our own oil and natural gas needs. The only hindrance is our own government. I have included at the back of this book the entire article by Stephen Moore of the Wall Street Journal. This article is an interview with Harold Hamm, who helped discover the Bakken oil fields in North Dakota. The following is a portion of Stephen Moore's story and Interview with Harold Hamm;

Washington keeps "sticking a regulatory boot at our necks and then turns around and asks: 'Why aren't you creating more jobs,'" he says. He roils at the Interior Department delays of months and sometimes years to get permits for drilling.

"These delays kill projects," he says. Even the Securities and Exchange Commission is now tightening the screws on the oil industry, requiring companies like Continental to report their production and federal royalties on thousands of individual leases under the Sarbanes-Oxley accounting rules. "I could go to jail because a local operator misreported the production in the field," he says.

The White House proposal to raise $40 billion of taxes on oil and gas—by excluding those industries from credits that go to all domestic manufacturers—is also a major hindrance to exploration and drilling. "That just stops the drilling," Mr. Hamm believes. "I've seen these things come about before, like [Jimmy] Carter's windfall profits tax." He says America's rig count on active wells went from 4,500 to less than 55 in a matter of months. "That was a dumb idea. Thank God, Reagan got rid of that."

A few months ago the Obama Justice Department brought charges against Continental and six other oil companies in North Dakota for causing the death of 28 migratory birds, in violation of the Migratory Bird Act. Continental's crime was killing one bird "the size of a sparrow" in its oil pits. The charges carry criminal penalties of up to six months in jail. "It's not even a rare bird. There're jillions of them," he explains. He says that "people in North Dakota are really outraged by these legal actions," which he views as "completely discriminatory" because the feds have rarely if ever prosecuted the Obama administration's beloved wind industry, which kills hundreds of thousands of birds each year.

Continental pleaded not guilty to the charges last week in federal court. For Mr. Hamm the whole incident is tantamount to harassment. "This shouldn't happen in America," he says. To him the case is further proof that Washington "is out to get us."

Mr. Hamm believes that if Mr. Obama truly wants more job creation, he should study North Dakota, the state with the lowest unemployment rate in the nation at 3.5%. He swears that number is overstated: "We can't find *any* unemployed people up there. The state has 18,000 unfilled jobs," Mr. Hamm insists. "And these are jobs that pay $60,000 to $80,000 a year." The economy is expanding so fast that North Dakota has a housing shortage. Thanks to the oil boom—Continental pays more than $50 million in state taxes a year— the state has a budget surplus and is considering ending income and property taxes.

It's hard to disagree with Mr. Hamm's assessment that Barack Obama has the energy story in America wrong. The government floods green energy—a niche market that supplies 2.5% of our energy needs—with billions of dollars of subsidies a year. "Wind isn't commercially feasible with natural gas prices below $6" per thousand cubic feet, notes Mr. Hamm. Right now its price is below $4. This may explain the administration's hostility to the fossil-fuel renaissance.

Mr. Hamm calculates that if Washington would allow more drilling permits for oil and natural gas on federal lands and federal waters, "I truly believe the federal government could over time raise $18 trillion in royalties." That's more than the U.S. national debt, I say. He smiles.

This estimate sounds implausibly high, but Mr. Hamm has a lifelong habit of proving skeptics wrong. And even if he's wrong by half, it's a stunning number to think about. So this America-first energy story isn't just about jobs and economic revival. It's also about repairing America's battered balance sheet. Someone should get this man in front of the congressional deficit-reduction supercommittee.[42]

Our own Democratic Party has blocked efforts to drill in ANWR in Alaska. This coastal plain can produce billions of barrels of oil. Using this source would result in lower dependence on foreign oil and would create an estimated 500,000 jobs- not just any jobs, but well paying jobs: it would also create billions of dollars of revenues from taxes and leases, dollars that would go directly to the local, state, and national government. However because ANWR is on a Protected Wilderness area, it needs Congressional approval. Guess who is apposed to drilling in ANWR, our own Democratic leaders in Congress. I would hope they want us to go back to work, to have less dependency on foreign oil, to have cheaper gas prices; however, they vote against the very things that could help. We simply can no longer support or vote for Democrats or Republicans that declare a need to free our country from foreign oil imports and then block all efforts to get our own oil. This would be like you or me owning 5,000 acres of land, needing desperately to eat, and yet deciding not to plant and grow any food because we wish to leave our land untouched, even though we have all the seeds, farm equipment and water available. We could feed, not just our family, but twenty families, and we could do it with just 50 acres, leaving

---

42   How North Dakota Became Saudi Arabia, by Stephen Moore, WSJ. Oct. 1, 2011

4,950 acres untouched. Does this make any sense? No, but that is exactly what is happening with our oil supply in America.

In 2008 Alaskan's received over $3,000 per resident as an annual dividend and payments from oil revenues the state acquired from land leases and taxes to oil companies. Similar payments to residents of Alaska have continued every year since 1976. Alaska receives billions of dollars every year as it uses its natural resources to provide income for the state and its residents. In addition, improvements in oil extraction have made the recovery process in Alaska very clean.[43]

Idaho is also cultivating one of its natural, renewable recourses, not oil but trees. The cultivation and replanting of Idaho's forests provides great paying jobs and millions of dollars directed to the educations of its citizens. In the last ten years, over 500 million dollars has gone to schools in Idaho from revenue of logging on private and state owned land. The best part about it is that as they log, they plant twice as many trees and return in 20 years to harvest again. Idaho could generate even more income and great paying jobs for its state, but most of its productive timberland is owned by the federal government and can not be harvested.[44] Alaska has the same problem; ANWAR and other oil reserves are on federal land, so it cannot be tapped for oil cultivation and exploration.

The federal government, in fact, owns (unconstitutionally) much of the Western U.S. land. Consequently, States cannot cultivate resources in their own state that would help create revenue and jobs in that state. For example, 84% of Nevada is federally owned, followed by 69% of Alaska, 57% of Utah, 53% of Oregon, 50% of Idaho, 48% of Arizona, 45% of California, 42% of Wyoming, 41% of New Mexico, and almost 37% of Colorado. Most of these states have huge amounts of oil, shale oil, coal, natural gas, forests, and other energy and job producing natural

---

43   The Seattle Times, by Angel Gonzallez and Hal Bernton

44   http://idahoforests.org, Idaho's working forests.

resources that could work to our advantage but cannot be acquired because of our own federal government. The Constitution does provide the right of the Federal Government to own state land for post offices, federal law enforcement offices and military instillations, but does not give the government the right to apprehend vast amounts of land to protect it; the state has that right, not the federal government.

A smaller, wiser, more efficient government would let the individual states cultivate, produce, use, and export any resources it has. We do this in our own families; we use all the resources we have to provide all the necessities we need and the many luxuries we enjoy. If we crashed our car in an accident and we had previously set aside more than enough money to purchase a new vehicle, we would most assuredly use that resource to purchase another car. It would be lunacy to call our employer and tell him or her we cannot get to work because we refuse to use our set aside resources to purchase a new or used car. We do not run our lives in such a ridiculous manner, and we must demand, via our votes, that the federal government does not run America in such a ridiculous manner. Our survival depends on using all these resources that have been given us. Use them responsibly, yes, but still use them. They have been placed there for us to use.

We have discussed just a few topics of big (Socialist) government; many more topics remain for discussion such as crushing regulations, high taxes, waste, corruption, enacted laws via unelected officials, and many more. We will, however discuss some of these issues as we cover the second, third, and fourth legs of the current Democratic party, which are redistribution of wealth, global warming and abortion.

CHAPTER 8

REDISTRIBUTION OF WEALTH, CLASS WARFARE, PUNISHING SUCCESS

In a recent Associated Press report, it was reported that almost half (47%) of the American people escape income taxes. The following is a portion of that story by Stephen Ohlemacher:

> "The result is a tax system that exempts almost half the country from paying for programs that benefit everyone, including national defense, public safety, infrastructure and education. It is a system in which the top 10 percent of earners – households making an average of $366,400 in 2006 – paid about 73 percent of the income taxes collected by the federal government.
>
> The bottom 40 percent, on average, makes a profit from the federal income tax, meaning they get more money in tax credits than they would otherwise owe in taxes. For those people, the government sends them a payment.

> "We have 50 percent of people who are getting something for nothing," said Curtis Dubay, senior tax policy analyst at the Heritage Foundation.[45]

In fact, if you count the rich as those people with incomes of $200,000 or more, they pay 85% of all the income taxes. In the interest of full disclosure, I will say that for most of my life, I have been part of that 40% of families that profit from the federal income tax. The tax and spend policy of our government is clearly not working. We tax the rich to death, and then our Democrat party denigrates them to death. Then, to punish them even more, we increase their taxes more because it simply is not fair that they are rich and we are poor. It is hard to believe that 10% of Americans pay for 73% of income taxes.[46] That, to me, is the part that is not fair. Even more astonishingly, some in the Democrat party say they should pay even more. How much more? Should they give the government all their income? I suppose that would at least get them in a lower tax bracket. Our own President Obama is continually saying that the rich just need to pay their fair share. It seems to me that they are paying way more than their fair share and should be praised instead of denigrated. We must not tax the successful out of prosperity. I have never seen a poor person employ anyone. Only successful people hire others; as those others become successful, they hire others. We in America want and need very successful, very profitable people and businesses so more people become employed and successful. That is, *THE AMERICAN DREAM.*"

I know most Democrats do not hate the rich; we all would like to be successful. I certainly would like to be more successful, but it seems as though elected officials in the Democrat party truly despise those in our country who have been and are very successful. We need not vote for such individuals that pit those who are rich against those who are poor. I believe the best friend of poverty is wealth, not government. Those in poverty exit poverty

---

45 The Associated Press, by Stephen Ohlemacher, April 7, 2010
46 The Associated Press, by Stephen Ohlemacher, April 7, 2010

only through success and wealth. The higher the taxes, the fewer wealthy people we have; thus, the greater number of poor people.

President John F. Kennedy knew this to be true. In his speech on Dec. 14th 1962 he said,

> "The final and best means of strengthening demand among consumers and business is to reduce the burden on private income and the deterrents to private initiative which are imposed by our present tax system — and this administration pledged itself last summer to an across-the-board, top-to-bottom cut in personal and corporate income taxes to be enacted and become effective in 1963.
>
> "I'm not talking about a "quickie" or a temporary tax cut, which would be more appropriate if a recession were imminent. Nor am I talking about giving the economy a mere shot in the arm, to ease some temporary complaint. I am talking about the accumulated evidence of the last five years that our present tax system, developed as it was, in good part, during World War II to restrain growth, exerts too heavy a drag on growth in peace time; that it siphons out of the private economy too large a share of personal and business purchasing power; that it reduces the financial incentives [sic] for personal effort, investment, and risk-taking. In short, to increase demand and lift the economy, the federal government's most useful role is not to rush into a program of excessive increases in public expenditures, but to expand the incentives and opportunities for private expenditures." He further said, "For all these reasons, next year's tax bill should reduce personal as well as corporate income taxes: for those in the lower brackets, who are certain to spend their additional take-home pay, and for those in the middle

and upper brackets, who can thereby be encouraged to undertake additional efforts and enabled to invest more capital." Later in that speech, he said, "In short, it is a paradoxical truth that tax rates are too high today and tax revenues are too low and the soundest way to raise the revenues in the long run is to cut the rates now. The experience of a number of European countries and Japan have borne this out. This country's own experience with tax reduction in 1954 has borne this out. And the reason is that only full employment can balance the budget, and tax reduction can pave the way to that employment. The purpose of cutting taxes now is not to incur a budget deficit, but to achieve the more prosperous, expanding economy which can bring a budget surplus.[47]"

The redistribution of wealth always creates more poor, not more wealthy; whereas, lower taxes and lower regulation always create more wealth and more revenue for the American people and the government. This then is truly a WIN-WIN. We must never punish success with higher taxes. As proof of this Leslie Kwoh, from the Star-Ledger Feb. 4, 2010, reported,

"More than $70 billion in wealth left New Jersey between 2004 and 2008 as affluent residents moved elsewhere, according to a report released Wednesday that marks a swift reversal of fortune for a state once considered the nation's wealthiest." "This was not always the case. The study – the first on interstate wealth migration in the country — noted the state actually saw an influx of $98 billion in the five years preceding 2004. The exodus of wealth, then, local experts and economists concluded, was a reaction to a series of changes in the

---

47   John F Kennedy, Dec. 14th 1962

state's tax structure — including increases in the income, sales, property and "millionaire" taxes.

"This study makes it crystal clear that New Jersey's tax policies are resulting in a significant decline in the state's wealth," said Dennis Bone, chairman of the New Jersey Chamber of Commerce and president of Verizon New Jersey. Wealthy residents are a key driver for everything from job creation and consumer spending to the real estate market and the state budget, said Jim Hughes, dean of the Edward J. Bloustein School of Planning and Public Policy at Rutgers University. In New Jersey, the top 1 percent of taxpayers pay more than 40 percent of the state's income tax. That's probably why we have these massive income shortfalls in the state budget, especially this year. Until the tax structure is improved," he said, "We'll probably see a continuation of the trend, until there are no more high-wealth individuals left."[48]

This condition is what occurs when we punish the rich: they leave, their money leaves, and then there is no money to help the poor. Our corporate tax rates in the US are the highest in the industrial world, not to mention the massive regulation heaped upon them. No wonder they need to lay off workers to make ends meet. Yet Democrats see a need to bash big business as evil and greedy. I am not saying that all private business is as clean and pure as the wind-driven snow, but I think if we take a good look at business as a whole we will find that they are much more honest, less greedy, and less corrupt than our federal government.

In a Wall Street Journal article by Arthur Laffer and Stephen Moore dated May 18, 2009, they reviewed research by Ohio University's Richard Vedder and found that from 1998 to 2007 Americans in large numbers have fled from high income tax

---

48   The Star Ledger, by Leslie Kwoh, Feb. 4, 2010

states to states with low or no income taxes. Over that same time period, the states with no income taxes created 89% more jobs and had 32% faster income growth than the states with income taxes. The article is aptly titled, "Soak the Rich, Lose the Rich." It cannot be said any better than that.

I would like to tell a personal story of a conversation I had some years ago with a very good friend of mine. He was a school teacher and perhaps one of the kindest, most Christ-like individuals I have ever known. He would help anyone who needed help; he did not live an extravagant life; how could he? He was a school teacher. I had him and his family over for dinner one night and we must have been discussing something to do with wealth or the government or business. To my astonishment, he declared his belief that the government should have a program to redistribute the income from the wealthy to the less fortunate population. I was amazed at his view. I hardly knew what to say; I tried to explain to him that this would make everyone poor and take away incentives to progress and succeed. I struggled in my arguments, and I do not think I was successful in changing his mind.

As I thought of this experience, I have tried to think of a better way to relate my point of view. As my friend was a school teacher, I think he could better understand how devastating the redistribution of wealth is to our country by how devastating such a practice would be in his classroom or school. Let's say he awarded all the failing students with an A and, in turn, gave the exceptional students a failing grades. He could easily argue that the failing students just did not have the time, intellect, and family circumstances available to them that the exceptional students had. He may explain that it was no fault of their own; this was just life's lottery, and they should not be punished with bad grades. They should be given a help up with the good grades of the other students. In turn, why should the exceptional students receive A's? They have won life's lottery! They should be more than happy to give their good grades to the failing students to help them out. Right?

This, concept is of course, ludicrous. The exceptional students could, of their own free will, choose to tutor the failing students to help them out, but the fact is that the A students worked, and worked hard for the grades they rightfully deserve. The failing students, more than likely, did not work as hard. It is true, some do not have the intellect that others have and would have a hard time getting good grades, but taking what one has rightfully earned and giving it to another who has not earned is theft and upsets the whole school program. Would anyone go to that school if this were the practice? What would the morale be of that class or school? Why try hard to get good grades? In fact, if I fail, I can get the "A" grade of another student. This fact is true unless of course, every student stops working for the "A" grade. Then there will be no "A's" to go around. The "B" grades would be the next to get redistributed to the failing students until the "B" students also stop trying. On it goes; get the picture? Then what would be the likelihood of success in higher education of those failing students that were given the A grades?

Some socialists would say we just want to even things out; we want everyone to be equal. Let's say my teacher friend simply decided to make all grades equal by awarding all the A and B students a C grade and also awarding the D and F students the same C grade. Again the result is the same as the previous example. Everyone stops trying. They already know what grade they will get regardless of effort. Everyone really fails. This is what socialism is: a failure formula, as Dr. Skousen would say. Dr. Skousen has also said, "Our Constitution does not provide the equal distribution of things, but the equal distribution of freedom and opportunity."

What about the poor in our country? We just cannot stand by and let the poor struggle along on their own. Shouldn't we take from the rich and give to the poor so they do not suffer? In a paper written by Robert Rector and Rachel Sheffield of the Heritage Foundation, research finds that in America the poor are not actually poor. They have cable TV, air conditioning, televisions; many have more than two televisions. The poor in America also have stoves, dishwashers, microwaves, washers and dryers, cell phones, and video games for the kids. In addition they have money to cover essential food, clothing and medical needs.[49]

I have traveled a little outside the U.S. and have seen what poverty really looks like, and it's nothing like poverty here in America. I have seen large neighborhoods; if you could call them that, that had bits of cardboard and metal scrapped together to make a shelter, no running water, no air conditioning, and certainly no televisions, refrigerators or microwave's. I am not saying we want poverty in America, we most certainly do not, clearly poverty does not exist in America as it does in many other countries around the world, and that's largely because of the vast amounts of wealth in our country. We have freedom to earn and keep what we earn, take that away and poverty will soon be knocking at our door.

America is a country of excellence, and we are the most prosperous, most powerful, and most giving of any country in the world; that is because of our Constitution, our values, our freedoms, and our hard work. We have been rewarded. If we stop the rewards, the excellence, the prosperity, the charity, and the freedoms will also stop; it upsets the whole program.

A John Stossel report, very clearly show the folly of wealth redistribution, here is a portion of his report:

September 29, 2010

Taxing the Rich

By **John Stossel**

Progressives want to raise taxes on individuals who make more than $200,000 a year because

---

49 Air Conditioning, Cable TV, and an Xbox: What is Poverty in the United States Today?, July 18, 2011 by Robert Rector and Rachel Sheffield.

they say it's wrong for the rich to be "given" more money. Sunday's New York Times carries a cartoon showing Uncle Sam handing money to a fat cat. They just don't get it.

As I've said before, a tax cut is not a handout. It simply means government steals less. What progressives want to do is take money from some – by force – and spend it on others. It sounds less noble when plainly stated.

That's the moral side of the matter. There's a practical side, too. Taxes discourage wealth creation. That hurts everyone, the lower end of the income scale most of all. An economy that, through freedom, encourages the production of wealth raises the living standards of lower-income people as well as everyone else.

A free society is not a zero-sum game in which every gain is offset by someone's loss. As long as government keeps its thumb off the scales, the "makers" who get rich do so by making others better off. (When the government allocates capital or creates barriers to competition, all bets are off.)

Of course, this is not the prevailing view among the intelligentsia. Columbia University Professor Marc Lamont Hill tells me, "Those who have more should pay more."

But is there a point where they stop producing wealth or leave altogether?

"The rich have always cried wolf like that," Hill says.

But the wolf is here. Maryland created a special tax on rich people that was supposed to bring in $106 million. Instead, the state lost $257 million.

Former Gov. Robert Ehrlich, who is running again for his old job, says: "It reminds me of Charlie

Brown. Charlie Brown was always surprised when Lucy pulled the football away. And they're always surprised in Washington and state capitals when the dollars never come in."

Some of Maryland's rich left the state. "They're out of here. These people aren't stupid," Ehrlich says.

New York billionaire Tom Golisano isn't stupid, either. With $3,000 and one employee, he started a business that processes paychecks for companies. He created 13,000 jobs.

Then New York state hiked the income tax on millionaires.

"It was the straw that broke the camel's back," he says. "Not that I like to throw the number around, but my personal income tax last year would've been $13,800 a day. Would you like to write a check for $13,800 a day to a state government, as opposed to moving to another state where there's no state income tax or very low state income tax?

He established residence in Florida, which has no personal income tax.

Now Gov. David Paterson may have even seen the light.

"We projected that we would get $4 billion, and we actually got well short of it," he says.

Art Laffer, the economist who has a curve illustrating this point named after him, isn't surprised.

"It's just economics," he says. "People don't work to pay taxes. People work to get what they can after tax. They'll change where they earn their income. They'll change how they earn their income. They'll change how much they earn, when they receive the income. They'll change all of those things to minimize taxes."

We can see it in the statistics. In 1960, federal revenues were 18.6 percent of total output. Over the next 50 years, that percentage has rarely exceeded 20 percent or fallen below 17 percent. As Laffer says, people adjust their activities to the tax burden.

Donald Trump, who knows something about making money, says of course the rich will leave when hit with higher taxes. "I know these people," he told me. "They're international people. Whether they live here or live in a place like Switzerland doesn't really matter to them."

You haven't left, I told him.

"I haven't left yet. ... Look, the rich people are going to leave. And other people are going to leave. You're going to end up with lots of people that don't produce. And then that's the spiral. That's the end."

And that's another good reason for us to get on with reducing the size of government."

Our party must start rewarding success instead of punishing it. The Democratic Party must not spread poverty, but spread opportunity. The more we punish success and tax prosperity out of America, the more people will flee our party and flee America. Previously, I discussed some of the current conditions in Venezuela. The most devastating results of the Socialist takeover of Venezuela is the fact that the all the wealthy have fled and have taken their money with them. Now there are much fewer jobs than before. Like it or not, the wealthy always do the hiring- always.

Wynn CEO, and prominent Democrat, Steve Wynn spelled it out clearly when he said the fallowing on a company conference call.

"I believe in Las Vegas. I think its best days are ahead of it. But I'm afraid to do anything in the current political environment in the United States. You watch television and see what's going on on this debt ceiling issue. And what I consider to be a total lack of leadership from the President and nothing's going to get fixed until the President himself steps up and wrangles both parties in Congress. But everybody is so political, so focused on holding their job for the next year that the discussion in Washington is nauseating.

And I'm saying it bluntly, that this administration is the greatest wet blanket to business, and progress and job creation in my lifetime. And I can prove it and I could spend the next 3 hours giving you examples of all of us in this market place that are frightened to death about all the new regulations, our healthcare costs escalate, regulations coming from left and right. A President that seems, that keeps using that word redistribution. **Well, my customers and the companies that provide the vitality for the hospitality and restaurant industry, in the United States of America, they are frightened of this administration**. And it makes you slow down and not invest your money. Everybody complains about how much money is on the side in America.

You bet and until we change the tempo and the conversation from Washington, it's not going to change. And those of us who have business opportunities and the capital to do it are going to sit in fear of the President. And a lot of people don't want to say that. They'll say, God, don't be attacking Obama. Well, this is Obama's deal and it's Obama that's responsible for this fear in America.

The guy keeps making speeches about redistribution and maybe we ought to do something to businesses that don't invest, their holding too much money. We haven't heard that kind of talk except from pure socialists. Everybody's afraid of the government and there's no need soft peddling it, it's the truth. It is the truth. And that's true of Democratic businessman and Republican businessman, and I am a Democratic businessman and I support Harry Reid. I support Democrats and Republicans. And I'm telling you that the business community in this company is frightened to death of the weird political philosophy of the President of the United States. And until he's gone, everybody's going to be sitting on their thumbs."[50]

---

50   Businessinsider.com by Joe Weisenthal, July 18th 2011

CHAPTER 9

GLOBAL WARMING-RADICAL ENVIRONMENTALISM

The third leg, or principle, of the current Democrat party is Radical Environmentalism, some call it Man Made Global Warming. I call it Climatism.

We will go over the vast evidence that thwarts the whole man made global warming theory, it's very important to know that the man made global warming theory, is just that- a theory. The current president of the Czech Republic, Vaclav Klaus, an economist and former citizen of Communism. In a letter to Congress he said:

> *"As someone who lived under communism for most of my life I feel obliged to say that the biggest threat to freedom, democracy, the market economy and prosperity at the beginning of the 21ˢᵗ century is not communism or its various softer variants. Communism* (has been) *replaced by the threat of ambitious environmentalism ..... The environmentalists consider their ideas and arguments to be an undisputable truth and use sophisticated methods of media manipulation and PR campaigns to exert pressure on policymakers to achieve their goals. Their argumentation is based on the spreading of fear and panic by declaring the future of the world to be under serious threat. In*

such an atmosphere they continue pushing policymakers to adopt illiberal measures, impose arbitrary limits, regulations, prohibitions, and restrictions on everyday human activities and make people subject to omnipotent bureaucratic decision-making. ... Man-made climate change has become one of the most dangerous arguments aimed at distorting human efforts and public policies in the whole world". [51]

President Klaus believes that radical environmentalism is the new home of communism and has stated that modern radical environmentalism is a great threat to freedom and prosperity. This is nothing new. Back in the early 20th century, Hitler and his Third Reich, as well as many Marxists, had a huge radical environmental program that crushed business, capitalism, and freedom.

In a story by Kevin Eggers, the Communist party in 1928 bannered a bold global environmental program to control all natural resources. They felt if they could get the citizens to give up freedoms to save nature then the government would control all the resources thus controling the people.[52]

The following is a portion of Kevin Eggers' report. "Why did the communists want a global environmental program?"

> "It's simple. Whomever controls resources controls people. If these con artists could convince citizens that mankind was just another animal destroying the environment, and that the only solution was their bureaucratic handlers controlling land and resources, what kind of lifestyle would citizens be willing to live to save the Earth?

---

51   letter to congress March, 2007, scienceandpublicpolicy.org, by Bob Carter, Thursday, 19 July 2007
52   Kevin Eggers, Napa Valley Register, Nov. 18,2009

From the Soviet Union's 1977 Constitution: "In the interests of the present and future generations, the necessary steps are taken ... to protect and make scientific, national use of the land and its mineral and water resources, and the plant and animal kingdoms to preserve the purity of air and water, ensure reproduction of natural wealth, and improve human development." Soviet con artists believe improving human development means controlling every aspect of it.

In "Earth in the Balance," Al Gore wrote that we should "use every policy and program, every law and institution, every treaty and alliance, every tactic and strategy, every plan and course of action — to use, in short, every means to halt the destruction of the environment and the preserve and nurture our ecological system." Would Gore's ends-justify-the-means environmental agenda include a film and Nobel Peace Prize?

Lord Christopher Monckton, former science advisor for British Prime Minister Margaret Thatcher, was influential in the British court ruling that requires teachers showing Gore's film "An Inconvenient Truth" to call it a "political work" and describe nine blatant falsehoods in the film. Monckton is now warning about the United Nations Climate Change Conference in Copenhagen, Dec. 7-18. According to Monckton, attendees will use "global warming hype" to sign what he believes will be an "institutional framework for an un-elected supreme communist-style world government."

Last May, I spoke with Holly Swanson, author of *Set Up and Sold Out*: Find Out What Green Really Means." Swanson, an environmental activist for 10 years before researching her book, told me the environmental movement had been politically "hijacked" and our government's "sustainable" solutions to environmental problems are intended to lead America into "communism."

"Set Up and Sold Out" references United Nations Agenda 21, which was signed onto by President H.W. Bush at the UN Rio Earth Summit in 1992, and implemented by the Clinton administration in 1993. Using fear of climate change and overpopulation, Agenda 21 essentially calls for international control over land use, resources and population. According to Rep. Ron Paul, R-Texas, both the Republican and Democratic parties are fully behind Agenda 21. Every federal agency is under Agenda 21 "sustainable" directives (including education), and there is a "master plan" for every county in the United States."[53]

As was mentioned, the 1977 Soviet constitution integrated a vast environmental plan to save the planet; instead, it was used to control the people and take away their freedoms. It did nothing for the environment; they were the worst polluters of all. In fact, the Black sea became so polluted that hardly anything could grow.

All environmentalists are not communists. However, I believe that our current Democratic party has moved so far left that it is approaching communism, and one of its tools to do so is the modern environmental movement. Many studies have shown that the more prosperous, free, and wealthy a nation is, the cleaner the environment is in that nation.

Professor Gabriel Calzada has produced a report with devastating economic news for Spain and the rest of the world concerning green jobs. Spain has a very aggressive green jobs plan, but at what cost? Each green job costs $752,000 to $1.4 million for each job, and at the same time each new green job results

---

53   Kevin Eggers, Napa Valley Register, Nov. 18th 2009

in the loss of 2.2 other jobs. This plan amounts to a net loss of 110,000 jobs over 8 years. Spain's unemployment is over 18% and growing. Is their environment cleaner or better then most other nations? No, but they do have a significant loss of freedoms and higher unemployment than most other nations.

Bjorn Lomborg said, "Work on research and development that will make new energy sources fully competitive with fossil fuels. And once they are you won't need a conference and treaties to force countries to be cleaner."[54]

He is right. Set the people free, and we will find the better, cheaper, and even cleaner solution.

Some say that climate change or global warming is the cause of so much poverty in the world, so it must be stopped. Lomborg has also addressed this issue saying,

> "Large scale aid to the world's poorest is no longer popular. So the world's advocates for the poor are just redrafting their demand, using climate change instead."[55] He also states that the majority of the problems of the world poor are not caused by climate change; they are caused by simple poverty. He says, "Every time we can save one person from dying from malnutrition through climate change policies, the same amount of money spent on malnutrition policies could save 5,000 people."[56]

I recently watched a speech by Dr. Patrick Moore, co-founder and former President of Greenpeace. He spoke on the environment, sustainable energy, and environmentalism. He said that Greenpeace did much good through the 1970's and half way through the 80's, but he had to leave the movement because of radical environmentalists' infiltration of the organization. He

---

54   PBS News Hour, Dec. 15, 2009
55   PBS News Hour Dec. 15, 2009
56   PBS News Hour Dec. 15,2009

stated two reasons for this. First, as reasonable issues were brought to light and policies changed, those that wanted to remain anti-establishment forever needed to move to more extremes and move away from science and fact. Secondly, as cold war communism fell, the far left needed a forum for their agenda. Dr Moore further states that extreme environmentalists are actually anti-human in their thinking. They believe that nature would be better off without the human race. In his view, they are also anti-science, anti-technology, anti-trade, anti-business, anti-capitalism, anti-profits, and anti-civilization. He further explains that 100 years ago the average human lifespan was only 35 years. (Today it is 77years). In Dr. Moore's view, the environmental movement should be based on correct science and fact.

The following Wall Street Journal article by Kimberley Stressel speaks for itself:

> "Steve Fielding recently asked the Obama administration to reassure him on the science of man-made global warming. When the administration proved unhelpful, Mr. Fielding decided to vote against climate-change legislation."

> "If you haven't heard of this politician, it's because he's a member of the Australian Senate. As the U.S. House of Representatives prepares to pass a climate-change bill, the Australian Parliament is preparing to kill its own country's carbon-emissions scheme. Why? A growing number of Australian politicians, scientists and citizens once again doubt the science of human-caused global warming."

> "Among the many reasons President Barack Obama and the Democratic majority are so intent on quickly jamming a cap-and-trade system through Congress is because the global warming tide is again shifting. It turns out Al Gore and the United Nations (with an assist from the media),

did a little too vociferous a job smearing anyone who disagreed with them as "deniers." The backlash has brought the scientific debate roaring back to life in Australia, Europe, Japan and even, if less reported, the U.S.

In April, the Polish Academy of Sciences published a document challenging man-made global warming. In the Czech Republic, where President Vaclav Klaus remains a leading skeptic, today only 11% of the population believes humans play a role. In France, President Nicolas Sarkozy wants to tap Claude Allegre to lead the country's new ministry of industry and innovation. Twenty years ago Mr. Allegre was among the first to trill about man-made global warming, but the geochemist has since recanted. New Zealand last year elected a new government, which immediately suspended the country's weeks-old cap-and-trade program.

The number of skeptics, far from shrinking, is swelling. Oklahoma Sen. Jim Inhofe now counts more than 700 scientists who disagree with the U.N. – 13 times the number who authored the U.N.'s 2007 climate summary for policymakers. Joanne Simpson, the world's first woman to receive a Ph.D. in meteorology, expressed relief upon her retirement last year that she was finally free to speak "frankly" of her nonbelief. Dr. Kiminori Itoh, a Japanese environmental physical chemist who contributed to a U.N. climate report, dubs man-made warming "the worst scientific scandal in history." Norway's Ivar Giaever, Nobel Prize winner for physics, decries it as the "new religion." A group of 54 noted physicists, led by Princeton's Will Happer, is demanding the American Physical Society revise its position that the science is settled. (Both Nature and Science magazines have refused to run the physicists' open letter.)

The collapse of the "consensus" has been driven by reality. The inconvenient truth is that the earth's temperatures have flat-lined since 2001, despite growing concentrations of CO_2. Peer-reviewed research has debunked doomsday scenarios about the polar ice caps, hurricanes, malaria, extinctions, rising oceans. A global financial crisis has politicians taking a harder look at the science that would require them to hamstring their economies to rein in carbon.

Credit for Australia's own era of renewed enlightenment goes to Dr. Ian Plimer, a well-known Australian geologist. Earlier this year he published "Heaven and Earth," a damning critique of the "evidence" underpinning man-made global warming. The book is already in its fifth printing. So compelling is it that Paul Sheehan, a noted Australian columnist – and ardent global warming believer – in April humbly pronounced it "an evidence-based attack on conformity and orthodoxy, including my own, and a reminder to respect informed dissent and beware of ideology subverting evidence." Australian polls have shown a sharp uptick in public skepticism; the press is back to questioning scientific dogma; blogs are having a field day.

The rise in skepticism also came as Prime Minister Kevin Rudd, elected like Mr. Obama on promises to combat global warming, was attempting his own emissions-reduction scheme. His administration was forced to delay the implementation of the program until at least 2011, just to get the legislation through Australia's House. The Senate was not so easily swayed.

Mr. Fielding, a crucial vote on the bill, was so alarmed by the renewed science debate that he made a fact-finding trip to the U.S., attending the Heartland Institute's annual conference for climate skeptics. He also visited with Joseph Aldy, Mr. Obama's special assistant on energy and the environment, where he challenged the Obama team to address his doubts. They apparently didn't.

This week Mr. Fielding issued a statement: He would not be voting for the bill. He would not risk job losses on "unconvincing green science." The bill is set to founder as the Australian parliament breaks for the winter.

Republicans in the U.S. have, in recent years, turned ever more to the cost arguments against climate legislation. That's made sense in light of the economic crisis. If Speaker Nancy Pelosi fails to push through her bill, it will be because rural and Blue Dog Democrats fret about the economic ramifications. Yet if the rest of the world is any indication, now might be the time for U.S. politicians to re-engage on the science. One thing for sure: They won't be alone."[57]

More and more scientists and climatologists are unconvinced every day. There is vast evidence that temperatures have been cooling for the last ten years. Dr. Moore reports cooling temps for the last twelve years at the same time CO_2 emissions are climbing. The fact is: CO_2 is critical for all life; there would not be any life on earth without it. CO_2 is an essential ingredient in the growth of plants and crops. Dr Moore estimates that CO_2 levels are very low compared to millions of years ago. He believes that we are still in an ice age as opposed to a greenhouse age that our earth has enjoyed most of its existence.

---

[57]   The Climate Change Climate Change, by Kimberley Stressel, June 26th 2009 WSJ.

To my surprise. I found a report from the U.S. Senate Committee on Environment and Public Works that reveals over 700 prominent international scientists have dissented from the man-made global warming fiasco. Some scientists in this report, reject the idea that carbon dioxide may be responsible for global warming. Many are calling the UN IPCC deceptive in its practices of global warming science.

The following are just a few of the comments from this report, http//epw.senate.gov

"I am a skeptic...Global warming has become a new religion."- Nobel Prize Winner for Physics, Ivar Giaever.

"Since I am no longer affiliated with any organization nor receiving any funding, I can speak quite frankly....As a scientist I remain skeptical...The main basis of the claim that man's release of greenhouse gases is the cause of the warming is based almost entirely upon climate models. We all know the frailty of models concerning the air-surface system." - Atmospheric Scientist Dr. Joanne Simpson, the first woman in the world to receive a PhD in meteorology, and formerly of NASA, who has authored more than 190 studies and has been called "among the most preeminent scientists of the last 100 years

Warming fears are the "worst scientific scandal in the history...When people come to know what the truth is, they will feel deceived by science and scientists." - UN IPCC Japanese Scientist Dr. Kiminori Itoh, an award-winning PhD environmental physical chemist.

"The IPCC has actually become a closed circuit; it doesn't listen to others. It doesn't have open minds... I am really amazed that the Nobel Peace Prize has been given on scientifically incorrect conclusions by people

who are not geologists." - Indian geologist Dr. Arun D. Ahluwalia at Punjab University and a board member of the UN-supported International Year of the Planet.

"So far, real measurements give no ground for concern about a catastrophic future warming." - Scientist Dr. Jarl R. Ahlbeck, a chemical engineer at Abo Akademi University in Finland, author of 200 scientific publications and former Greenpeace member.

"Even doubling or tripling the amount of carbon dioxide will virtually have little impact, as water vapour and water condensed on particles as clouds dominate the worldwide scene and always will." – . Geoffrey G. Duffy, a professor in the Department of Chemical and Materials Engineering of the University of Auckland, NZ.

Anyone who claims that the debate is over and the conclusions are firm has a fundamentally unscientific approach to one of the most momentous issues of our time." - Solar physicist Dr. Pal Brekke, senior advisor to the Norwegian Space Centre in Oslo. Brekke has published more than 40 peer-reviewed scientific articles on the sun and solar interaction with the Earth.

"The models and forecasts of the UN IPCC "are incorrect because they only are based on mathematical models and presented results at scenarios that do not include, for example, solar activity." - Victor Manuel Velasco Herrera, a researcher at the Institute of Geophysics of the National Autonomous University of Mexico

"It is a blatant lie put forth in the media that makes it seem there is only a fringe of scientists who don't buy into anthropogenic global warming." - U.S Government Atmospheric Scientist Stanley B.

Goldenberg of the Hurricane Research Division of NOAA

"The Kyoto theorists have put the cart before the horse. It is global warming that triggers higher levels of carbon dioxide in the atmosphere, not the other way round...A large number of critical documents submitted at the 1995 U.N. conference in Madrid vanished without a trace. As a result, the discussion was one-sided and heavily biased, and the U.N. declared global warming to be a scientific fact," Andrei Kapitsa, a Russian geographer and Antarctic ice core researcher.

I am convinced that the current alarm over carbon dioxide is mistaken...Fears about man-made global warming are unwarranted and are not based on good science." - Award Winning Physicist Dr. Will Happer, Professor at the Department of Physics at Princeton University and Former Director of Energy Research at the Department of Energy, who has published over 200 scientific papers, and is a fellow of the American Physical Society, The American Association for the Advancement of Science, and the National Academy of Sciences.

"The quantity of CO2 we produce is insignificant in terms of the natural circulation between air, water and soil... I am doing a detailed assessment of the UN IPCC reports and the Summaries for Policy Makers, identifying the way in which the Summaries have distorted the science." - South Afican Nuclear Physicist and Chemical Engineer Dr. Philip Lloyd, a UN IPCC co-coordinating lead author who has authored over 150 refereed publications.

"Many [scientists] are now searching for a way to back out quietly (from promoting warming fears), without having their professional careers ruined." -

Atmospheric physicist James A. Peden, formerly of the Space Research and Coordination Center in Pittsburgh.

"Creating an ideology pegged to carbon dioxide is a dangerous nonsense...The present alarm on climate change is an instrument of social control, a pretext for major businesses and political battle. It became an ideology, which is concerning." - Environmental Scientist Professor Delgado Domingos of Portugal, the founder of the Numerical Weather Forecast group, has more than 150 published articles.

"CO2 emissions make absolutely no difference one way or another....Every scientist knows this, but it doesn't pay to say so...Global warming, as a political vehicle, keeps Europeans in the driver's seat and developing nations walking barefoot." - Dr. Takeda Kunihiko, vice-chancellor of the Institute of Science and Technology Research at Chubu University in Japan.

"The 'global warming scare' is being used as a political tool to increase government control over American lives, incomes and decision making. It has no place in the Society's activities." - Award-Winning NASA Astronaut/Geologist and Moonwalker Jack Schmitt who flew on the Apollo 17 mission and formerly of the Norwegian Geological Survey and for the U.S. Geological Survey.

"Earth has cooled since 1998 in defiance of the predictions by the UN-IPCC....The global temperature for 2007 was the coldest in a decade and the coldest of the millennium...which is why 'global warming' is now called 'climate change.'" - Climatologist Dr. Richard Keen of the Department of Atmospheric and Oceanic Sciences at the University of Colorado

All I can say is "WOW!" I did not know that! Our Democrat party continues to push a cap and trade bill that will cripple our economy and our freedoms, all based on man-made global warming. Democrats cannot simply ignore the facts; we must not sell our freedoms for fear.

There is additional evidence of man making up man-made global warming, such as the University of East Anglia's Climate Research Unit's e-mails, revealing the falsification of temperatures, also known as "Climate-gate" and the many studies showing cooling, instead of warming.

The modern extreme environmental movement seeks to fleece America of both its prosperity and its freedoms in the effort to "Save the Planet".

This leg of man-made global warming and extreme environmentalism is a leg I do not want the Democratic Party to be resting on. It moves us toward socialism, and I believe most Democrats do not live this way. We love clean air and water; everyone does. The fact is that in America we have made great strides in clean air and water because of our freedoms. Our prosperity has given us the financial capital to do so. Poor and/or socialist countries cannot make these advances in cleaning the environment because they simply have more pressing matters, such as food and survival.

Amazingly some, (mostly the leadership of the Democrat party and the extreme environmental wing of the party), will go to great lengths to protect an endangered habitat, animal, or rodent (perhaps rightly so), but will at the same time go to even greater lengths to kill innocent unborn babies. This brings us to the last, and I think most devastating, leg of our party platform; Abortion.

CHAPTER 10

ABORTION

A few facts and statistics first:

1.2 million abortions recorded in America per year. www.nric.org

53 million abortions performed since 1973. www.nric.org

60% of Americans oppose abortion except in rare cases of incest or rape. www.lifenews.com

75% of Americans do not support the current on-demand abortion policies. – Gallup Poll, May 2009, mccl.org

51% of Hispanics oppose abortion, LifeNews.com, story by Steven Ertelt, Sept. 6,2007

42% of Blacks oppose abortion, LifeNews.com. by Steven Ertelt, Sept. 6, 2007

only 13% of Americans believe in legal abortion under any circumstance, Gallup Poll May 5, 2005

67% of Americans believe in Legal abortion only under certain circumstances, Gallup Poll, May 5, 2005

51% of Americans call themselves Pro-life, 42% call themselves Pro-choice. Gallup Poll, May 2009.

71% of all Americans think late term or partial birth abortion should be illegal. Gallup Poll, May 2007.

68% of Republican consider themselves Pro-life, 34% of Democrat women consider themselves Pro-life. Gallup Poll, May 2010

"75% do not support the current abortion-on-demand policy, saying abortion should be legal only in some circumstances (53%), or illegal in all circumstances (22%).

Gallup Poll, May 2009

78% believe that women who have abortions commonly experience moderately severe to very severe negative emotional reactions to abortion.

Medical Science Monitor, 2003

95% of women want to be informed of all risks of a medical procedure; 69% want to be informed of all alternatives.

Journal of Medical Ethics, July 2006

64% of women who experienced one or more abortions "felt pressured by others" to have the abortion.

Medical Science Monitor, Oct. 2004" [58]

Why do women have abortions?

74% say having a baby would interfere with work, school, or other responsibilities.

73% say they cannot afford to have a child.

48% say they do not want to be a single parent, or have relationship problems with husband or partner.

Less than 2% say they became pregnant as a result of rape or incest.

Source: The Alan Guttmacher In. www.mcci.org/ Page.aspx?pid=400

A Zogby poll in 2004 showed that a majority of Americans oppose 96% of all abortions. And 78% of Hispanics support a pro-life position and 62% of Blacks support a pro-life position. 74% of Americans said that taxpayer money should not be used to pay for abortions.

THE HUMAN HEART BEGINS TO BEAT 18-21 DAYS AFTER FERTILIZATION.

I was one day listening to a radio program (the Dr. Laura show); she was discussing unwanted pregnancy, and she made a

---

58   www.mcci.org/Page.aspx?pid=400

comment that at first shocked me. She said, "Do we consider killing the mother after an unwanted pregnancy occurs? No, then why do we kill an innocent baby after an unwanted pregnancy occurs?" This comment made me realize that abortion is simply illogical, (as Spock would say). Abortion does not make any sense.

On the euthanasia.com web site, it states that one of the reasons we do not have any abortion positions from President Kennedy, or any one else prior to the 1960's is because It was not even thought of; it was illegal and immoral. It was considered an abhorrent crime, a crime of the worst kind, killing an innocent baby.[59] What have we become?. Adoption is and should always be the best solution for unwanted pregnancies.

What about the woman's right to choose? All women, and men for that matter, have the right to choose, especially in America. This fact is what makes America so special. In America we have more freedom to choose than in any other country in the world; up until the last 20 to 30 years, we have for the most part made good choices. We also have a constitution; we are ruled by a set of laws, not by the "whims of Man". Women have the right to choose unprotected sex, and to choose pregnancy or not, unless incest or rape is the means of that pregnancy, but the instant a women is pregnant, she is carrying another human being who is protected by the American constitution: *Life, Liberty, and the Pursuit of Happiness.* Adoption is the leg on which the Democrat party should rest, not on ripping an innocent baby limb from limb and then sucking the baby into a sink to die!

These babies are the most pure and innocent members of our society. The Democrat party hails itself as the party that stands for the little guy, the party of those without a voice, the party that helps those who cannot help themselves. Yet the most helpless, innocent, and voiceless among us, we seek to torture and kill when to choose otherwise would simply be inconvenient. If the Democrat party were truly the party for the little guy, the party that helps the

---

59   www.euthanasis.com/presidentkenney.html

helpless, we would praise, teach, plead and advocate ADOPTION, not abortion. In some areas of our country a 14 year old girl in school cannot get a couple of aspirin for a headache without a parent's permission. However, that same girl can be hurried off to kill her unwanted baby without her parents knowing anything about it, and our Democrat party is largely responsible. Thousands, perhaps hundreds of thousands, of loving, nurturing, capable couples wait and wait for the chance to adopt and care for a child, yet our own Democrat party champions slaughter over salvation, for the most helpless and pure among us. This is DISGUSTING; we should be ashamed of abortion, not praising it.

Unfortunately, we have a president that is a strong proponent of on-demand abortions and even partial birth abortions. President Obama's own appointee, John Holdren, advocates forced abortions, seizing young mother's babies, and mass sterilization. [60]

We can do better. We must do better. Most Democrats would choose adoption over abortion if they had to make the choice. Most Americans oppose abortion. Most minority groups oppose abortion, yet many of us continue to vote for Democrats that seek the killing of innocent life at all costs. We must VOTE THE WAY WE LIVE. This is one of the best ways we can take back our Democratic party. We must vote for those that are pro-life not pro-death. We must support, teach, plead, and advocate adoption for unwanted babies. We should fervently oppose abortion unless the pregnancy is the result of rape, incest or in cases where the mother's life is in danger. In cases of rape or incest the "woman's right to choose" has already been taken away.

We must return to the party that stands up for the little guy; we can surely stand up for innocent babies and give them a voice for life, freedom, and a future with a loving family.

---

60   Ecoscience,, 1977 by John Holdren and Paul Ehrlich. www.thetruthwins.com

CHAPTER II

A New Platform for the Democrat Party "A Time For Choosing"

I am sure many reading this book will be wondering, "What should we stand for as a party?" If we have the character to abandon the current platform of Big Government, Redistribution of Wealth, Radical Environmentalism and Abortion, what will be our platform?

The answers are actually very simple to state but very difficult to do. After many years of plotting along the socialist path, we must reverse the course and walk another path. Fortunately for us, it is a path we have been on before, a path that always leads to success, freedom, prosperity, stability, safety, and strength. That path, in two words, is CONSERVATISM and CAPITALISM. It is of course the modern term for what our founders and most people the world over used to call THE AMERICAN WAY. It is also known as the PRINCIPLES OF FREEDOM. These principles of freedom are universal. They work every time they are tried, and they work for any nation or people that applies them. These principles are small, efficient, limited government, low taxation, low regulation, freedom to try, buy, sell, and fail, rewarding success, and standing up for human life. Our U.S. Declaration of Independence states this very clearly, "Life, Liberty, and the Pursuit of Happiness."

It will not be enough just to stand for such principles; we as Democrats, must, as we did in the past, lead the way. We cannot rely on others to do so. The Republicans do have many in their party that are true conservatives, but for some reason they have a hard time leading the way. Our Democratic party, on the other hand, seems more comfortable in the role of leadership. Unfortunately for America, for the past twenty years or so, we have been leading in the wrong direction. America as a whole, and for that matter, Democrats as a whole, live conservative lives. However the Democrat leadership has been leading our party and our nation swiftly toward socialism, and socialism, as Dr. Skousen would say, is a "failure formula." We need conservative Democrats to run and win elected offices; conservatism, capitalism and our Constitution is and always will be a success formula. We as Democrats must never put the D in front of the conservative American principle we live by. The only way to truly take back our party is to vote the way we live, even if that means to vote for some one from a different party. If such a person believes what we believe, and if he/she lives the way we live, then he or she is worthy of our vote, regardless of party. The current Tea Party Movement is an example of Democrats, Independents, and Republicans joining forces in protest of big socialist government policies and principles.

We can also use the Kennedy senate seat in Massachusetts as a good example of how to vote the way we live. Massachusetts is 75% Democrat, but they voted for the conservative Republican. They have had personal experience with socialized medicine and seen the devastation it has brought to their state; they did not want that for the country. They simply voted the way they lived. This particular senate seat has been in liberal hands for over 40 years, but the people have seen what socialism has done, and they took a stand. This is true leadership. Democrats also lead the way to the Republican Bob Turner winning the Ninth Congressional District in NY. This New York District is overwhelmingly a Democrat district, by over three to one. A Republican has not held this District in almost 90 years. But Democrats lead the way, and again took a stand against the socialist pattern of our current president. In Arizona, the people have been devastated by the lack of backbone from the federal government to enforce immigration laws so they are doing it themselves. It's time to stand for what we believe. The Democrat party has a rich history in leadership and values, a history we must now return to in order to take back our country and our party

Turning back to the question, what platform should the Democrat party adopt? Perhaps we can take a look at the 1932 Democrat platform to give us a few suggestions.

Democratic Party Platform of 1932

"In this time of unprecedented economic and social distress the Democratic Party declares its conviction that the chief causes of this condition were the disastrous policies pursued by our government since the World War, of economic isolation, fostering the competitive businesses into monopolies and encouraging the indefensible expansion and contraction of credit for private profit at the expense of the public.

Those who were responsible for these policies have abandoned the ideals on which the war was won and thrown away the fruits of victory, thus rejecting the greatest opportunity in history to bring peace, prosperity, and happiness to our people and to the world.

They have ruined our foreign trade; destroyed the values of our commodities and products, crippled our banking system, robbed millions of our people of their life savings, and thrown millions more out of work, produced wide-spread poverty and brought the government to a state of financial distress unprecedented in time of peace.

The only hope for improving present conditions, restoring employment, affording permanent relief to the people, and bringing the nation back to the proud position of domestic happiness and of financial, industrial, agricultural and commercial leadership in the world lies in a drastic change in economic governmental policies.

We believe that a party platform is a covenant with the people to have [sic] faithfully kept by the party when entrusted with power, and that the people are entitled to know in plain words the terms of the contract to which they are asked to subscribe. We hereby declare this to be the platform of the Democratic Party:

The Democratic Party solemnly promises by appropriate action to put into effect the principles, policies, and reforms herein advocated, and to eradicate the policies, methods, and practices herein condemned. We advocate an immediate and drastic reduction of governmental expenditures by abolishing useless commissions and offices, consolidating departments and bureaus, and eliminating extravagance to accomplish a saving of not less than twenty-five per cent in the cost of the Federal Government. And we call upon the Democratic Party in the states to make a zealous effort to achieve a proportionate result.

We advocate a sound currency to be preserved at all hazards and an international monetary conference called on the invitation of our government to consider the reha. We advocate a Navy and an Army adequate for national defense, based on a survey of all facts affecting the existing establish-ments, that the people in time of peace may not be burdened by an expenditure fast approaching a bil-lion dollars annually bilitation of silver and related questions.

We advocate strengthening and impartial en-forcement of the anti-trust laws, to prevent monop-oly and unfair trade practices, and revision thereof for the better protection of labor and the small producer and distributor.

The conservation, development, and use of the nation's water power in the public interest.

The removal of government from all fields of private enterprise except where necessary to devel-op public works and natural resources in the com-mon interest.

We advocate protection of the investing pub-lic by requiring to be filed with the government and carried in advertisements of all offerings of foreign and domestic stocks and bonds true in-formation as to bonuses, commissions, principal invested, and interests of the sellers."[61]

In all fairness, I have included just some of the Democratic platform of 1932. Some of this platform is more leftist and slight-ly socialist, but it clearly states many conservative ideas and sound ideas of smaller, less intrusive government, of a government with a balanced budget- spending only what it has and not squander-ing its revenue.

We can go back to a more conservative, Constitutional, capi-talist platform. A platform of : Downsizing government by 30% instead of increasing government by 30%; a platform of lower-ing Taxes and government regulation by at least 30% instead of increasing taxes and regulations; a platform of rewarding success

---

61   1932 Democratic Party Platform

via a fair tax system, instead of massive high taxation for those who are successful. We can support a platform of choosing, via school vouchers, the schools our kids attend, instead of forcing kids into failing schools; a platform of using our own energy resources instead of foreign oil; a platform of a balanced budget, spending only what we have instead of spending more than even our great, great, great grandchildren will be able to pay back; a platform of adoption instead of abortion; a platform of strength instead of weakness; a platform of freedom instead of socialism; a platform more aligned with the way most of us live; a platform more aligned with the Democrat party of old, States' rights and LIMITED FEDERAL GOVERNMENT.

The recent 2010 midterm elections showed us that most Americans, including Democrats, want smaller more conservative government. Republicans in the House of Representatives won 63 seats, the largest gain in over 70 years. Republicans also made gains in the Senate, not to mention the massive gains in state elections. They did it running on repealing national health care, controlling spending, and lowering taxes. Every once in a while, we test the waters of socialism, and in short order we see the disaster of its floods. Accordingly, we quickly move to higher ground. Make no mistake about it: the midterm elections of 2010 was our country moving to higher ground.

Democrats need now to continue to move towards the higher ground of FREEDOM and CAPITALISM, and smaller more efficient ethical government.

As we elect more Democrats who desire less government, less taxes, less regulation, we will be voting the way we live. We are in large part a conservative nation, a nation that has brought great success to us as individuals and as a nation. We have seen from 2008 to 2012 that the Progressive pattern of socialism and big government simply does not work; it brings disaster at every turn. It has also brought disaster to the Democratic Party. The Democrat Party is so infiltrated with extreme liberal, socialist, and progressive people and views that it will continue to decrease in size and relevancy until we return it back to the great party it used to be: a party that fought for freedoms, for values, for country, for the American Way, and the American Dream.

Thomas Jefferson, the founder of the Democratic Party, said "A wise and frugal government, which shall leave men free to regulate their own pursuits of industry and improvement, and shall not take from the mouth of labor the bread it has earned - this is the sum of good government."

As was mentioned in the beginning of this work, the American Democrat Party is Americas Party. It has obligations to the American people to lead our country towards freedom, prosperity, and the American way. The majority of Democrats in America have great values of faith, frugality, honesty, integrity, hard work, and service to others. The current Democratic leadership does not seem to have these same values. We must not serve the party; the party must serve us. Our Democrat Party must now turn from importing socialism and poverty to exporting prosperity and freedom. It is truly a time for choosing.

We must now:

VOTE THE WAY WE LIVE, AND TAKE BACK OUR DEMOCRAT PARTY.

CHAPTER 12

A TIME FOR CHOOSING

Reagan's speech, Oct. 27th 1964 <u>Reagan</u>: Thank you. Thank you very much. Thank you and good evening. The sponsor has been identified, but unlike most television programs, the performer hasn't been provided with a script. As a matter of fact, I have been permitted to choose my own words and discuss my own ideas regarding the choice that we face in the next few weeks.

I have spent most of my life as a Democrat. I recently have seen fit to follow another course. I believe that the issues confronting us across party lines. Now, one side in this campaign has been telling us that the issues of this election are the maintenance of peace and prosperity. The line has been used, "We've never had it so good."

But I have an uncomfortable feeling that this prosperity isn't something on which we can base our hopes for the future. No nation in history has ever survived a tax burden that reached a third of its national income. Today, 37 cents out of every dollar earned in this country is the tax collector's share, and yet our government continues to spend 17 million dollars a day more than the government takes in. We haven't balanced our budget 28 out of the last 34 years. We've raised our debt limit three times in the last twelve months, and now our national debt is one and a half times bigger than all the combined debts of all the nations of the world. We have 15 billion dollars in gold in our treasury; we don't own an ounce. Foreign dollar claims are 27.3 billion dollars. And we've just had announced that the dollar of 1939 will now purchase 45 cents in its total value.

As for the peace that we would preserve, I wonder who among us would like to approach the wife or mother whose husband or son has died in South Vietnam and ask them if they think this is a peace that should be maintained indefinitely. Do they mean peace, or do they mean we just want to be left in peace? There can be no real peace while one American is dying some place in the world for the rest of us. We're at war with the most dangerous enemy that has ever faced mankind in his long climb from the swamp to the stars, and it's been said if we lose that war, and in so doing lose this way of freedom of ours, history will record with the greatest astonishment that those who had the most to lose did the least to prevent its happening. Well I think it's time we ask ourselves if we still know the freedoms that were intended for us by the Founding Fathers.

Not too long ago, two friends of mine were talking to a Cuban refugee, a businessman who had escaped from Castro, and in the midst of his story one of my friends turned to the other and said, "We don't know how lucky we are." And the Cuban stopped and said, "How lucky you are? I had someplace to escape to." And in that sentence he told us the entire story. If we lose freedom here, there's no place to escape to. This is the last stand on earth.

And this idea that government is beholden to the people, that it has no other source of power except the sovereign people, is still the newest and the most unique idea in all the long history of man's relation to man.

This is the issue of this election: whether we believe in our capacity for self-government or whether we abandon the American revolution and confess that a little intellectual elite in a far-distant capitol can plan our lives for us better than we can plan them ourselves.

You and I are told increasingly we have to choose between a left or right. Well I'd like to suggest there is no such thing as a left or right. There's only an up or down: [up] man's old – old-aged dream, the ultimate in individual freedom consistent with law and order, or down to the ant heap of totalitarianism. And regardless of their sincerity, their humanitarian motives, those who would trade our freedom for security have embarked on this downward course.

In this vote-harvesting time, they use terms like the "Great Society," or as we were told a few days ago by the President, we must accept a greater government activity in the affairs of the people. But they've been a little more explicit in the past and among themselves; and all of the things I now will quote have appeared in print. These are not Republican accusations. For example, they have voices that say, "The cold war will end through our acceptance of a not undemocratic socialism." Another voice says, "The profit motive has become outmoded. It must be replaced by the incentives of the welfare state." Or, "Our traditional system of individual freedom is incapable of solving the complex problems of the 20th century." Senator Fulbright has said at Stanford University that the Constitution is outmoded. He referred to the President as "our moral teacher and our leader," and he says he is "hobbled in his task by the restrictions of power imposed on him by this antiquated document." He must "be freed," so that he "can do for us" what he knows "is best." And Senator Clark of Pennsylvania, another articulate spokesman, defines liberalism as "meeting the material needs of the masses through the full power of centralized government."

Well, I, for one, resent it when a representative of the people refers to you and me, the free men and women of this country, as "the masses." This is a term we haven't applied to ourselves in America. But beyond that, "the full power of centralized government" – this was the very thing the Founding Fathers sought to minimize. They knew that governments don't control things. A government can't control the economy without controlling people. And they know when a government sets out to do that, it must use force and coercion to achieve its purpose. They also knew, those Founding Fathers, that outside of its legitimate functions, government does nothing as well or as economically as the private sector of the economy.

Now, we have no better example of this than government's involvement in the farm economy over the last 30 years. Since 1955, the cost of this program has nearly doubled. One-fourth of farming in America is responsible for 85% of the farm surplus. Three-fourths of farming is out on the free market and has known a 21% increase in the per capita consumption of all its produce. You see, that one-fourth of farming – that's regulated and controlled by the federal government. In the last three years we've spent 43 dollars in the feed grain program for every dollar bushel of corn we don't grow.

Senator Humphrey last week charged that Barry Goldwater, as President, would seek to eliminate farmers. He should do his homework a little better, because he'll find out that we've had a decline of 5 million in the farm population under these government programs. He'll also find that the Democratic administration has sought to get from Congress [an] extension of the farm program to include that three-fourths that is now free. He'll find that they've also asked for the right to imprison farmers who wouldn't keep books as prescribed by the federal government. The Secretary of Agriculture asked for the right to seize farms through condemnation and resell them to other individuals. And contained in that same program was a provision that would have allowed the federal government to remove 2 million farmers from the soil.

At the same time, there's been an increase in the Department of Agriculture employees. There's now one for every 30 farms in the United States, and still they can't tell us how 66 shiploads of grain headed for Austria disappeared without a trace and <u>Billie Sol Estes</u> never left shore.

Every responsible farmer and farm organization has repeatedly asked the government to free the farm economy, but how – who are farmers to know what's best for them? The wheat farmers voted against a wheat program. The government passed it anyway. Now the price of bread goes up; the price of wheat to the farmer goes down.

Meanwhile, back in the city, under urban renewal the assault on freedom carries on. Private property rights [are] so diluted that public interest is almost anything a few government planners decide it should be. In a program that takes from the needy and gives to the greedy, we see such spectacles as in Cleveland, Ohio, a million-and-a-half-dollar building completed only three years ago must be destroyed to make way for what government officials call a "more compatible use of the land." The President tells us he's now going to start building public housing units in the thousands, where heretofore we've only built them in the hundreds. But FHA [Federal Housing Authority] and the Veterans Administration tell us they have 120,000 housing units they've taken back through mortgage foreclosure. For three decades, we've sought to solve the problems of unemployment through government planning, and the more the plans fail, the more the planners plan. The latest is the Area Redevelopment Agency.

They've just declared Rice County, Kansas, a depressed area. Rice County, Kansas, has two hundred oil wells, and the 14,000 people there have over 30 million dollars on deposit in personal savings in their banks. And when the government tells you you're depressed, lie down and be depressed.

We have so many people who can't see a fat man standing beside a thin one without coming to the conclusion the fat man got that way by taking advantage of the thin one. So they're going to solve all the problems of human misery through government and government planning. Well, now, if government planning and welfare had the answer – and they've had almost 30 years of it – shouldn't we expect government to read the score to us once in a while? Shouldn't they be telling us about the decline each year in the number of people needing help? The reduction in the need for public housing?

But the reverse is true. Each year the need grows greater; the program grows greater. We were told four years ago that

17 million people went to bed hungry each night. Well that was probably true. They were all on a diet. But now we're told that 9.3 million families in this country are poverty-stricken on the basis of earning less than 3,000 dollars a year. Welfare spending [is] 10 times greater than in the dark depths of the Depression. We're spending 45 billion dollars on welfare. Now do a little arithmetic, and you'll find that if we divided the 45 billion dollars up equally among those 9 million poor families, we'd be able to give each family 4,600 dollars a year. And this added to their present income should eliminate poverty. Direct aid to the poor, however, is only running only about 600 dollars per family. It would seem that someplace there must be some overhead.

Now – so now we declare "<u>war on poverty</u>," or "You, too, can be a Bobby Baker." Now do they honestly expect us to believe that if we add 1 billion dollars to the 45 billion we're spending, one more program to the 30-odd we have – and remember, this new program doesn't replace any, it just duplicates existing programs – do they believe that poverty is suddenly going to disappear by magic? Well, in all fairness I should explain there is one part of the new program that isn't duplicated. This is the youth feature. We're now going to solve the dropout problem, juvenile delinquency, by reinstituting something like the old <u>CCC camps</u> [Civilian Conservation Corps], and we're going to put our young people in these camps. But again we do some arithmetic, and we find that we're going to spend each year just on room and board for each young person we help 4,700 dollars a year. We can send them to Harvard for 2,700! Course, don't get me wrong. I'm not suggesting Harvard is the answer to juvenile delinquency.

But seriously, what are we doing to those we seek to help? Not too long ago, a judge called me here in Los Angeles. He told me of a young woman who'd come before him for a divorce. She had six children, was pregnant with her seventh. Under his questioning, she revealed her husband was a laborer earning 250 dollars a month. She wanted a divorce to get an 80 dollar raise. She's eligible for 330 dollars a month in the Aid to Dependent Children

Program. She got the idea from two women in her neighborhood who'd already done that very thing.

Yet anytime you and I question the schemes of the do-gooders, we're denounced as being against their humanitarian goals. They say we're always "against" things – we're never "for" anything.

Well, the trouble with our liberal friends is not that they're ignorant; it's just that they know so much that isn't so.

Now – we're for a provision that destitution should not follow unemployment by reason of old age, and to that end we've accepted Social Security as a step toward meeting the problem.

But we're against those entrusted with this program when they practice deception regarding its fiscal shortcomings, when they charge that any criticism of the program means that we want to end payments to those people who depend on them for a livelihood. They've called it "insurance" to us in a hundred million pieces of literature. But then they appeared before the Supreme Court and they testified it was a welfare program. They only use the term "insurance" to sell it to the people. And they said Social Security dues are a tax for the general use of the government, and the government has used that tax. There is no fund, because Robert Byers, the actuarial head, appeared before a congressional committee and admitted that Social Security as of this moment is 298 billion dollars in the hole. But he said there should be no cause for worry because as long as they have the power to tax, they could always take away from the people whatever they needed to bail them out of trouble. And they're doing just that.

A young man, 21 years of age, working at an average salary –his Social Security contribution would, in the open market, buy him an insurance policy that would guarantee 220 dollars a month at age 65. The government promises 127. He could live it up until he's 31 and then take out a policy that would pay more than Social Security. Now are we so lacking in business sense that we can't put this program on a sound basis, so that people who do require those payments will find they can get them when they're due – that the cupboard isn't bare?

Barry Goldwater thinks we can.

At the same time, can't we introduce voluntary features that would permit a citizen who can do better on his own to be excused upon presentation of evidence that he had made provision for the non-earning years? Should we not allow a widow with children to work, and not lose the benefits supposedly paid for by her deceased husband? Shouldn't you and I be allowed to declare who our beneficiaries will be under this program, which we cannot do? I think we're for telling our senior citizens that no one in this country should be denied medical care because of a lack of funds. But I think we're against forcing all citizens, regardless of need, into a compulsory government program, especially when we have such examples, as was announced last week, when France admitted that their Medicare program is now bankrupt. They've come to the end of the road.

In addition, was Barry Goldwater so irresponsible when he suggested that our government give up its program of deliberate, planned inflation, so that when you do get your Social Security pension, a dollar will buy a dollar's worth, and not 45 cents worth?

I think we're for an international organization, where the nations of the world can seek peace. But I think we're against subordinating American interests to an organization that has become so structurally unsound that today you can muster a two-thirds vote on the floor of the General Assembly among nations that represent less than 10 percent of the world's population. I think we're against the hypocrisy of assailing our allies because here and there they cling to a colony, while we engage in a conspiracy of silence and never open our mouths about the millions of people enslaved in the Soviet colonies in the satellite nations.

I think we're for aiding our allies by sharing of our material blessings with those nations which share in our fundamental beliefs, but we're against doling out money government to government, creating bureaucracy, if not socialism, all over the world. We set out to help 19 countries. We're helping 107. We've spent 146 billion dollars. With that money, we bought a 2 million dollar yacht for Haile Selassie. We bought dress suits for Greek under-takers, extra wives for Kenya[n] government officials. We bought a thousand TV sets for a place where they have no electricity. In the last six years, 52 nations have bought 7 billion dollars worth of our gold, and all 52 are receiving foreign aid from this country.

No government ever voluntarily reduces itself in size. So, governments' programs, once launched, never disappear.

Actually, a government bureau is the nearest thing to eternal life we'll ever see on this earth.

Federal employees – federal employees number two and a half million; and federal, state, and local, one out of six of the nation's work force employed by government. These proliferating bureaus with their thousands of regulations have cost us many of our constitutional safeguards. How many of us realize that today federal agents can invade a man's property without a warrant? They can impose a fine without a formal hearing, let alone a trial by jury? And they can seize and sell his property at auction to enforce the payment of that fine. In Chico County, Arkansas, James Wier over-planted his rice allotment. The government obtained a 17,000 dollar judgment. And a U.S. marshal sold his 960-acre farm at auction. The government said it was necessary as a warning to others to make the system work.

Last February 19th at the University of Minnesota, Norman Thomas, six-times candidate for President on the Socialist Party ticket, said, "If Barry Goldwater became President, he would stop the advance of socialism in the United States." I think that's exactly what he will do.

But as a former Democrat, I can tell you Norman Thomas isn't the only man who has drawn this parallel to socialism with the present administration, because back in 1936, Mr. Democrat himself, Al Smith, the great American, came before the American people and charged that the leadership of his Party was taking the Party of Jefferson, Jackson, and Cleveland down the road under the banners of Marx, Lenin, and Stalin. And he walked away from his Party, and he never returned 'til the day he died – because to this day, the leadership of that Party has been taking that Party, that honorable Party, down the road in the image of the labor Socialist Party of England.

Now it doesn't require expropriation or confiscation of private property or business to impose socialism on a people. What does it mean whether you hold the deed to the – or the title to your business or property if the government holds the power of life and death over that business or property? And such machinery already exists. The government can find some charge to bring against any concern it chooses to prosecute. Every businessman has his own tale of harassment. Somewhere a perversion has taken place. Our natural, unalienable rights are now considered to be a dispensation of government, and freedom has never been so fragile, so close to slipping from our grasp as it is at this moment.

Our Democratic opponents seem unwilling to debate these issues. They want to make you and I believe that this is a contest between two men – that we're to choose just between two personalities.

Well what of this man that they would destroy – and in destroying, they would destroy that which he represents, the ideas that you and I hold dear? Is he the brash and shallow and trigger-happy man they say he is? Well I've been privileged to know him "when." I knew him long before he ever dreamed of trying for high office, and I can tell you personally I've never known a man in my life I believed so incapable of doing a dishonest or dishonorable thing.

This is a man who, in his own business before he entered politics, instituted a profit-sharing plan before unions had ever thought of it. He put in health and medical insurance for all his employees. He took 50 percent of the profits before taxes and set up a retirement program, a pension plan for all his employees. He sent monthly checks for life to an employee who was ill and couldn't work. He provides nursing care for the children of mothers who work in the stores.

When Mexico was ravaged by the floods in the Rio Grande, he climbed in his airplane and flew medicine and supplies down there.

An ex-GI told me how he met him. It was the week before Christmas during the Korean War, and he was at the Los Angeles airport trying to get a ride home to Arizona for Christmas. And he said that [there were] a lot of servicemen there and no seats available on the planes. And then a voice came over the loudspeaker and said, "Any men in uniform wanting a ride to Arizona, go to runway such-and-such," and they went down there, and there was a fellow named Barry Goldwater sitting in his plane. Every day in those weeks before Christmas, all day long, he'd load up the plane, fly it to Arizona, fly them to their homes, fly back over to get another load.

During the hectic split-second timing of a campaign, this is a man who took time out to sit beside an old friend who was dying of cancer. His campaign managers were understandably impatient, but he said, "There aren't many left who care what happens to her. I'd like her to know I care." This is a man who said to his 19-year-old son, "There is no foundation like the rock of honesty and fairness, and when you begin to build your life on that rock, with the cement of the faith in God that you have, then you have a real start." This is not a man who could carelessly send other people's sons to war. And that is the issue of this campaign that makes all the other problems I've discussed academic, unless we realize we're in a war that must be won.

Those who would trade our freedom for the soup kitchen of the welfare state have told us they have a utopian solution of peace without victory. They call their policy "accommodation." And they say if we'll only avoid any direct confrontation with the enemy, he'll forget his evil ways and learn to love us. All who oppose them are indicted as warmongers. They say we offer simple answers to complex problems. Well, perhaps there is a simple answer – not an easy answer – but simple: If you and I have the courage to tell our elected officials that we want our national policy based on what we know in our hearts is morally right.

We cannot buy our security, our freedom from the threat of the bomb by committing an immorality so great as saying to a billion human beings now enslaved behind the <u>Iron Curtain</u>, "Give up your dreams of freedom because to save our own skins, we're willing to make a deal with your slave masters." Alexander Hamilton said, "A nation which can prefer disgrace to danger is prepared for a master, and deserves one." Now let's set the record straight. There's no argument over the choice between peace and war, but there's only one guaranteed way you can have peace – and you can have it in the next second – surrender.

Admittedly, there's a risk in any course we follow other than this, but every lesson of history tells us that the greater risk lies in appeasement, and this is the specter our well-meaning liberal friends refuse to face – that their policy of accommodation is appeasement, and it gives no choice between peace and war, only between fight or surrender. If we continue to accommodate, continue to back and retreat, eventually we have to face the final demand – the ultimatum. And what then – when Nikita Khrushchev has told his people he knows what our answer will be? He has told them that we're retreating under the pressure of the Cold War, and someday when the time comes to deliver the final ultimatum, our surrender will be voluntary, because by that time we will have been weakened from within spiritually, morally, and economically. He believes this because from our side he's heard voices pleading for "peace at any price" or "better Red than dead," or as one commentator put it, he'd rather "live on his knees than die on his feet." And therein lies the road to war, because those voices don't speak for the rest of us.

You and I know and do not believe that life is so dear and peace so sweet as to be purchased at the price of chains and slavery. If nothing in life is worth dying for, when did this begin – just in the face of this enemy? Or should Moses have told the children of Israel to live in slavery under the pharaohs? Should Christ have refused the cross? Should the patriots at Concord Bridge have thrown down their guns and refused to fire the shot heard 'round the world? The martyrs of history were not fools, and our honored dead who gave their lives to stop the advance of the Nazis didn't die in vain. Where, then, is the road to peace? Well it's a simple answer after all.

You and I have the courage to say to our enemies, "There is a price we will not pay." "There is a point beyond which they must not advance." And this – this is the meaning in the phrase of Barry Goldwater's "peace through strength." Winston Churchill said, "The destiny of man is not measured by material computations. When great forces are on the move in the world, we learn we're spirits – not animals." And he said, "There's something going on in time and space, and beyond time and space, which, whether we like it or not, spells duty."

You and I have a rendezvous with destiny.

We'll preserve for our children this, the last best hope of man on earth, or we'll sentence them to take the last step into a thousand years of darkness.

We will keep in mind and remember that Barry Goldwater has faith in us. He has faith that you and I have the ability and the dignity and the right to make our own decisions and determine our own destiny.

Thank you very much.

CHAPTER 13

KENNEDY'S SPEECH.

Address at the Economic Club of New York, December 14th, 1962

General Royall, Mr. Trippe, Mr. Rockefeller, General Clay, gentlemen:

I feel tonight somewhat like I felt when I addressed in 1960 the Houston Ministers Conference on the separation of church and state. But I am glad to have a chance to talk to you tonight about the advantages of the free enterprise system. [Applause]

Less than a month ago this Nation reminded the world that it possessed both the will and the weapons to meet any threat to the security of free men. The gains we have made will not be given up, and the course that we have pursued will not be abandoned. But in the long run, that security will not be determined by military or diplomatic moves alone. It will be affected by the decisions of finance ministers as well as by the decisions of Secretaries of State and Secretaries of Defense; by the deployment of fiscal and monetary weapons as well as by military weapons; and above all by the strength of this Nation's economy as well as by the strength of our defenses.

You will recall that Chairman Khrushchev has said that he believed that the hinge of world history would begin to move when the Soviet Union out-produced the United States. Therefore, the subject to which we address ourselves tonight concerns not merely our own well-being, but also very vitally the defense of the free world. America's rise to world leadership in the century since the Civil War has reflected more than anything else our unprecedented economic growth. Interrupted during the decade of the thirties, the vigorous expansion of our economy was resumed in 1940 and continued for more than 15 years thereafter. It demonstrated for all to see the power of freedom and the efficiency of free institutions. The economic health of this Nation has been and is now fundamentally sound.

But a leading nation, a nation upon which all depend not only in this country but around the world, cannot afford to be satisfied, to look back or to pause. On our strength and growth depend the strength of others, the spread of free world trade and unity, and continued confidence in our leadership and our currency. The underdeveloped countries are dependent upon us for the sale of their primary commodities and for aid to their struggling economies. In short, a prosperous and growing America is important not only to Americans–it is, as the spokesman for 20 Western nations in the Organization for Economic Cooperation and Development, as he stressed this week, of vital importance to the entire Western World.

In the last 2 years we have made significant strides. Our gross national product has risen 11 percent while inflation has been arrested. Employment has been increased by 1.3 million jobs. Profits, personal income, living standards–all are setting new records. Most of the economic indicators for this quarter are up and the prospects are for further expansion in the next quarter. But we must look beyond the next quarter, or the last quarter, or even the last 2 years. For we can and must do better, much better than we have been doing for the last 5 1/2 years.

This economy is capable of producing without strain $30 to $40 billion more than we are producing today. Business earnings could be $7 to $8 billion higher than they are today. Utilization of existing plant and equipment could be much higher; and if it were, investment would rise. We need not accept an unemployment rate Of 5 percent or more, such as we have had for 60 out of the last 61 months. There is no need for us to be satisfied with a rate of growth that keeps good men out of work and good capacity out of use.

The Economic Club of New York is of course familiar with these problems. For in this State the rate of insured unemployment has been persistently higher than the national average, and the increases in personal income and employment have been slower here than in the Nation as a whole. You have seen the tragedy of chronically depressed areas upstate, of unemployed young people, and I think this might be one of our most serious national problems, unemployed young people, those under 20, one out of four is unemployed, particularly those in the minority groups, roaming the streets of New York and our other great cities, and others on relief at an early age, with the prospect that in this decade we will have between 7 and 8 million school dropouts, unskilled, coming into the labor market, at a time when the need for unskilled labor is steadily diminishing. And I know you share my conviction that, proud as we are of its progress, this Nation's economy can and must do even better than it has done in the last 5 years. Our choice, therefore, boils down to one of doing nothing and thereby risking a widening gap between our actual and potential growth in output, profits, and employment-or taking action, at the Federal level, to raise our entire economy to a new and higher level of business activity.

If we do not take action, those who have the most reason to be dissatisfied with our present rate of growth will be tempted to seek shortsighted and narrow solutions–to resist automation, to reduce the work week to 35 hours or even lower, to shut out imports, or to raise prices in a vain effort to obtain full capacity profits on under-capacity operations. But these are all self-defeating expedients which can only restrict the economy, not expand it.

There are a number of ways by which the Federal Government can meet its responsibilities to aid economic growth. We can and must improve American education and technical training. We can and must expand civilian research and technology. One of the great bottlenecks for this country's economic growth in this decade will be the shortage of doctorates in mathematics, engineering, and physics; a serious shortage with a great demand and an under-supply of highly trained manpower. We can and must step up the development of our natural resources.

But the most direct and significant kind of Federal action aiding economic growth is to make possible an increase in private consumption and investment demand–to cut the fetters which hold back private spending. In the past, this could be done in part by the increased use of credit and monetary tools, but our balance of payments situation today places limits on our use of those tools for expansion. It could also be done by increasing Federal expenditures more rapidly than necessary, but such a course would soon demoralize both the Government and our economy. If Government is to retain the confidence of the people, it must not spend more than can be justified on grounds of national need or spent with maximum efficiency. I shall say more on this in a moment.

The final and best means of strengthening demand among consumers and business is to reduce the burden on private income and the deterrents to private initiative which are imposed by our present tax system; and this administration pledged itself last summer to an across-the-board, top-to-bottom cut in personal and corporate income taxes to be enacted and become effective in 1963.

I am not talking about a "quickie" or a temporary tax cut, which would be more appropriate if a recession were imminent. Nor am I talking about giving the economy a mere shot in the arm, to ease some temporary complaint. I am talking about the accumulated evidence of the last 5 years that our present tax system, developed as it was, in good part, during World War II to restrain growth, exerts too heavy a drag on growth in peace time; that it siphons out of the private economy too large a share of personal and business purchasing power; that it reduces the financial incentives for personal effort, investment, and risk-taking.

In short, to increase demand and lift the economy, the Federal Government's most useful role is not to rush into a program of excessive increases in public expenditures, but to expand the incentives and opportunities for private expenditures.

Under these circumstances, any new tax legislation–and you can understand that under the comity which exists in the United States Constitution whereby the Ways and Means Committee in the House of Representatives have the responsibility of initiating this legislation, that the details of any proposal should wait on the meeting of the Congress in January. But you can understand that under these circumstances, in general, that any new tax legislation enacted next year should meet the following three tests:

First, it should reduce net taxes by a sufficiently early date and a sufficiently large amount to do the job required. Early action could give us extra leverage, added results, and important insurance against recession. Too large a tax cut, of course, could result in inflation and insufficient future revenues–but the greatest danger is a tax cut too little or too late to be effective.

Second, the new tax bill must increase private consumption as well as investment. Consumers are still spending between 92 and 94 'percent of their after-tax income, as they have every year since 1950. But that after-tax income could and should be greater, providing stronger markets for the products of American industry. When consumers purchase more goods, plants use more of their capacity, men are hired instead of laid off, investment increases and profits are high.

Corporate tax rates must also be cut to increase incentives and the availability of investment capital. The Government has already taken major steps this year to reduce business tax liability and to stimulate the modernization, replacement, and expansion of our productive plant and equipment. We have done this through the 1962 investment tax credit and through the liberalization of depreciation allowances–two essential parts of our first step in tax revision which amounted to a 10 percent reduction in corporate income taxes worth $2.5 billion. Now we need to increase consumer demand to make these measures fully effective–demand which will make more use of existing capacity and thus increase both profits and the incentive to invest. In fact, profits after taxes would be at least 15 percent higher today if we were operating at full employment.

For all these reasons, next year's tax bill should reduce personal as well as corporate income taxes, for those in the lower brackets, who are certain to spend their additional take-home pay, and for those in the middle and upper brackets, who can thereby be encouraged to undertake additional efforts and enabled to invest more capital.

Third, the new tax bill should improve both the equity and the simplicity of our present tax system. This means the enactment of long-needed tax reforms, a broadening of the tax base and the elimination or modification of many special tax privileges. These steps are not only needed to recover lost revenue and thus make possible a larger cut in present rates; they are also tied directly to our goal of greater growth. For the present patchwork of special provisions and preferences lightens the tax load of some only at the cost of placing a heavier burden on others. It distorts economic judgments and channels an undue amount of energy into efforts to avoid tax liabilities. It makes certain types of less productive activity more profitable than other more valuable undertakings. All this inhibits our growth and efficiency, as well as considerably complicating the work of both the taxpayer and the Internal Revenue Service.

These various exclusions and concessions have been justified in part as a means of overcoming oppressively high rates in the upper brackets–and a sharp reduction in those rates, accompanied by base-broadening, loophole-closing measures, would properly make the new rates not only lower but also more widely applicable. Surely this is more equitable on both counts.

Those are the three tests which the right kind of bill must meet and I am confident that the enactment of the right bill next year will in due course increase our gross national product by several times the amount of taxes actually cut. Profit margins will be improved and both the incentive to invest and the supply of internal funds for investment will be increased. There will be new interest in taking risks, in increasing productivity, in creating new jobs and new products for long-term economic growth.

Other national problems, moreover, will be aided by full employment. It will encourage the location of new plants in areas of labor surplus and provide new jobs for workers that we are retraining and facilitate the adjustment which will be necessary under our new trade expansion bill and reduce a number of government expenditures.

It will not, I'm confident, revive an inflationary spiral or adversely affect our balance of payments. If the economy today were operating close to capacity levels with little unemployment, or if a sudden change in our military requirements should cause a scramble for men and resources, then I would oppose tax reductions as irresponsible and inflationary; and I would not hesitate to recommend a tax increase, if that were necessary. But our resources and manpower are not being fully utilized; the general level of prices has been remarkably stable; and increased competition, both at home and abroad, along with increased productivity will help keep both prices and wages within appropriate limits.

The same is true of our balance of payments. While rising demand will expand imports, new investment in more efficient productive facilities will aid exports and a new economic climate could both draw capital from abroad and keep capital here at home. It will also put us in a better position, if necessary, to use monetary tools to help our international accounts. But, most importantly, confidence in the dollar in the long run rests on confidence in America, in our ability to meet our economic commitments and reach our economic goals. In a worldwide conviction that we are not drifting from recession to recession with no answer, the substantial improvement in our balance of payments position in the last 2 years makes it clear that nothing could be more foolish than to restrict our growth merely to minimize that particular problem, because a slowdown in our economy will feed that problem rather than diminish it. On the contrary, European governmental and financial authorities with almost total unanimity, far from threatening to withdraw gold, have urged us to cut taxes in order to expand our economy, attract more capital, and increase confidence in our future.

But what concerns most Americans about a tax cut, I know, is not the deficit in our balance of payments but the deficit in our Federal budget. When I announced in April of 1961 that this kind of comprehensive tax reform would follow the bill enacted this year, I had hoped to present it in an atmosphere of a balanced budget. But it has been necessary to augment sharply our nuclear and conventional forces, to step up our efforts in space, to meet the increased cost of servicing the national debt and meeting our obligations, established by law, to veterans. These expenditure increases, let me stress, constitute practically all of the increases which have occurred under this administration, the remainder having gone to fight the recession we found in industry–mostly through the supplemental employment bill-and in agriculture.

We shall, therefore, neither postpone our tax cut plans nor cut into essential national security programs. This administration is determined to protect America's security and survival and we are also determined to step up its economic growth. I think we must do both.

Our true choice is not between tax reduction, on the one hand, and the avoidance of large Federal deficits on the other. It is increasingly clear that no matter what party is in power, so long as our national security needs keep rising, an economy hampered by restrictive tax rates will never produce enough revenue to balance our budget just as it will never produce enough jobs or enough profits. Surely the lesson of the last decade is that budget deficits are not caused by wild-eyed spenders but by slow economic growth and periodic recessions, and any new recession would break all deficit records.

In short, it is a paradoxical truth that tax rates are too high today and tax revenues are too low and the soundest way to raise the revenues in the long run is to cut the rates now. The experience of a number of European countries and Japan have borne this out. This country's own experience with tax reduction in 1954 has borne this out. And the reason is that only full employment can balance the budget, and tax reduction can pave the way to that employment. The purpose of cutting taxes now is not to incur a budget deficit, but to achieve the more prosperous, expanding economy which can bring a budget surplus.

I repeat: our practical choice is not between a tax-cut deficit and a budgetary surplus. It is between two kinds of deficits: a chronic deficit of inertia, as the unwanted result of inadequate revenues and a restricted economy; or a temporary deficit of transition, resulting from a tax cut designed to boost the economy, increase tax revenues, and achieve–and I believe this can be done–a budget surplus. The first type of deficit is a sign of waste and weakness; the second reflects an investment in the future.

Nevertheless, as Chairman Mills of the House Ways and Means Committee pointed out this week, the size of the deficit is to be regarded with concern, and tax reduction must be accompanied, in his words, by "increased control of the rises in expenditures." This is precisely the course we intend to follow in 1963.

At the same time as our tax program is presented to the Congress in January, the Federal budget for fiscal 1964 will also be presented. Defense and space expenditures will necessarily rise in order to carry out programs which are demanded and are necessary for our own security, and which have largely been authorized by Members in both parties of the Congress with overwhelming majorities. Fixed interest charges on the debt also rise slightly. But I can tell you now that the total of all other expenditures combined will be held at approximately its current level.

This is not an easy task. During the past 9 years, domestic civilian expenditures in the National Government have risen at an average rate of more than 71/2 percent. State and local government expenditures have risen at an annual rate of 9 percent. Expenditures by the New York State Government, for example, have risen in recent years at the rate of roughly 10 percent a year. At a time when Government pay scales have necessarily risen–and I take New York just as an example–when our population and pressures are growing and the demand for services and State aid is thus increasing, next year's Federal budget, which will hold domestic outlays at their present level, will represent a genuine effort in expenditure control. This budget will reflect, among other economies, a $750 million reduction in the postal deficit. It will reflect a savings of over $300 million in the storage costs of surplus feed grain stocks, and as a result of the feed grain bill of 1961 we will have two-thirds less in storage than we would otherwise have had in January 1963 and a savings of at least $600 million from the cancellation of obsolete or unworkable weapons systems. Secretary McNamara is undertaking a cost reduction program expected to save at least $3 billion a year in the Department of Defense, cutting down on duplication and closing down nonessential installations. Other agencies must do the same.

In addition, I have directed all heads of Government departments and agencies to hold Federal employment under the levels authorized by congressional appropriations; to absorb through greater efficiency a substantial part of this year's Federal pay increase; to achieve an increase in productivity which will enable the same amount of work to be done by fewer people; and to refrain from spending any unnecessary funds that were appropriated by the Congress.

It should also be noted that the Federal debt, as a proportion of our gross national product, has been steadily reduced in this last year. Last year the total increase in the Federal debt was 2 percent–compared to an 8 percent increase in the gross debt of State and local governments. Taking a longer view, the Federal debt today is 13 percent higher than it was in 1946, while State and local debt increased over 360 percent and private debt by over 300 percent. In fact, if it were not for Federal financial assistance to State and local governments, the Federal cash budget would show a surplus. Federal civilian employment, for example, is actually lower today than it was in 1952, while State and local government employment over the same period has increased 67 percent.

It is this setting which makes Federal tax reduction both possible and appropriate next year. I do not underestimate the obstacles which the Congress will face in enacting such legislation. No one will be satisfied. Everyone will have his own approach, his own bill, his own reduction. A high order of restraint and determination will be required if the possible is not to wait on the perfect. But a nation capable of marshaling these qualities in any dramatic threat to its security is surely capable, as a great free society, of meeting a slower and more complex threat to our economic vitality. This Nation can afford to reduce taxes, we can afford a temporary deficit, but we cannot afford to do nothing. For on the strength of our free economy rests the hope of all free nations. We shall not fail that hope, for free men and free nations must prosper and they must prevail.

Thank you

THE WALL STREET JOURNAL.

WSJ.com

OCTOBER 1, 2011

How North Dakota Became Saudi Arabia

By STEPHEN MOORE

Harold Hamm, the Oklahoma-based founder and CEO of Continental Resources, the 14th-largest oil company in America, is a man who thinks big. He came to Washington last month to spread a needed message of economic optimism: With the right set of national energy policies, the United States could be "completely energy independent by the end of the decade. We can be the Saudi Arabia of oil and natural gas in the 21st century."

"President Obama is riding the wrong horse on energy," he adds. We can't come anywhere near the scale of energy production to achieve energy independence by pouring tax dollars into "green energy" sources like wind and solar, he argues. It has to come from oil and gas.

You'd expect an oilman to make the "drill, baby, drill" pitch. But since 2005 America truly has been in the midst of a revolution in oil and natural gas, which is the nation's fastest-growing manufacturing sector. No one is more responsible for that resurgence than Mr. Hamm. He was the original discoverer of the gigantic and prolific Bakken oil fields of Montana and North Dakota that have already helped move the U.S. into third place among world oil producers.

How much oil does Bakken have? The official estimate of the U.S. Geological Survey a few years ago was between four and five billion barrels. Mr. Hamm disagrees: "No way. We estimate that the entire field, fully developed, in Bakken is 24 billion barrels."

If he's right, that'll double America's proven oil reserves. "Bakken is almost twice as big as the oil reserve in Prudhoe Bay, Alaska," he continues. According to Department of Energy data,

North Dakota is on pace to surpass California in oil production in the next few years. Mr. Hamm explains over lunch in Washington, D.C., that the more his company drills, the more oil it finds. Continental Resources has seen its "proved reserves" of oil and natural gas (mostly in North Dakota) skyrocket to 421 million barrels this summer from 118 million barrels in 2006.

"We expect our reserves and production to triple over the next five years." And for those who think this oil find is only making Mr. Hamm rich, he notes that today in America "there are 10 million royalty owners across the country" who receive payments for the oil drilled on their land. "The wealth is being widely shared."

One reason for the renaissance has been OPEC's erosion of market power. "For nearly 50 years in this country nobody looked for oil here and drilling was in steady decline. Every time the domestic industry picked itself up, the Saudis would open the taps and drown us with cheap oil," he recalls. "They had unlimited production capacity, and company after company would go bust."

Today OPEC's market share is falling and no longer dictates the world price. This is huge, Mr. Hamm says. "Finally we have an opportunity to go out and explore for oil and drill without fear of price collapse." When OPEC was at its peak in the 1990s, the U.S. imported about two-thirds of its oil. Now we import less than half of it, and about 40% of what we do import comes from Mexico and Canada. That's why Mr. Hamm thinks North America can achieve oil independence.

The other reason for America's abundant supply of oil and natural gas has been the development of new drilling techniques. "Horizontal drilling" allows rigs to reach two miles into the ground and then spread horizontally by thousands of feet. Mr. Hamm was one of the pioneers of this method in the 1990s, and it has done for the oil industry what hydraulic fracturing has done for natural gas drilling in places like the Marcellus Shale in the Northeast. Both innovations have unlocked decades worth of new sources of domestic fossil fuels that previously couldn't be extracted at affordable cost.

Mr. Hamm's rags to riches success is the quintessential "only in America" story. He was the last of 13 kids, growing up in rural Oklahoma "the son of sharecroppers who never owned land." He didn't have money to go to college, so as a teenager he went to work in the oil fields and developed a passion. "I always wanted to find oil. It was always an irresistible calling."

He became a wildcat driller and his success rate became legendary in the industry. "People started to say I have ESP," he remarks. "I was fortunate, I guess. Next year it will be 45 years in the business."

Mr. Hamm ranks 33rd on the Forbes wealth list for America, but given the massive amount of oil that he owns, much still in the ground, and the dizzying growth of Continental's output and profits (up 34% last year alone), his wealth could rise above $20 billion and he could soon be rubbing elbows with the likes of Warren Buffett.

His only beef these days is with Washington. Mr. Hamm was invited to the White House for a "giving summit" with wealthy Americans who have pledged to donate at least half their wealth to charity. (He's given tens of millions of dollars already to schools like Oklahoma State and for diabetes research.) "Bill Gates, Warren Buffett, they were all there," he recalls.

When it was Mr. Hamm's turn to talk briefly with President Obama, "I told him of the revolution in the oil and gas industry and how we have the capacity to produce enough oil to enable America to replace OPEC. I wanted to make sure he knew about this."

The president's reaction? "He turned to me and said, 'Oil and gas will be important for the next few years. But we need to go on to green and alternative energy. [Energy] Secretary [Steven] Chu has assured me that within five years, we can have a battery developed that will make a car with the equivalent of 130 miles per gallon.'" Mr. Hamm holds his head in his hands and says, "Even if you believed that, why would you want to stop oil and gas development? It was pretty disappointing."

Washington keeps "sticking a regulatory boot at our necks and then turns around and asks: 'Why aren't you creating more jobs,'" he says. He roils at the Interior Department delays of months and sometimes years to get permits for drilling. "These delays kill projects," he says. Even the Securities and Exchange Commission is now tightening the screws on the oil industry, requiring companies like Continental to report their production and federal royalties on thousands of individual leases under the Sarbanes-Oxley accounting rules. "I could go to jail because a local operator misreported the production in the field," he says.

The White House proposal to raise $40 billion of taxes on oil and gas—by excluding those industries from credits that go to all domestic manufacturers—is also a major hindrance to exploration and drilling. "That just stops the drilling," Mr. Hamm believes. "I've seen these things come about before, like [Jimmy] Carter's windfall profits tax." He says America's rig count on active wells went from 4,500 to less than 55 in a matter of months. "That was a dumb idea. Thank God, Reagan got rid of that."

A few months ago the Obama Justice Department brought charges against Continental and six other oil companies in North Dakota for causing the death of 28 migratory birds, in violation of the Migratory Bird Act. Continental's crime was killing one bird "the size of a sparrow" in its oil pits. The charges carry criminal penalties of up to six months in jail. "It's not even a rare bird. There're jillions of them," he explains. He says that "people in North Dakota are really outraged by these legal actions," which he views as "completely discriminatory" because the feds have rarely if ever prosecuted the Obama administration's beloved wind industry, which kills hundreds of thousands of birds each year.

Continental pleaded not guilty to the charges last week in federal court. For Mr. Hamm the whole incident is tantamount to harassment. "This shouldn't happen in America," he says. To him the case is further proof that Washington "is out to get us."

Mr. Hamm believes that if Mr. Obama truly wants more job creation, he should study North Dakota, the state with the lowest unemployment rate in the nation at 3.5%. He swears that number is overstated: "We can't find **any** unemployed people up there. The state has 18,000 unfilled jobs," Mr. Hamm insists. "And these are jobs that pay $60,000 to $80,000 a year." The economy is expanding so fast that North Dakota has a housing shortage. Thanks to the oil boom—Continental pays more than $50 million in state taxes a year—the state has a budget surplus and is considering ending income and property taxes.

It's hard to disagree with Mr. Hamm's assessment that Barack Obama has the energy story in America wrong. The government floods green energy—a niche market that supplies 2.5% of our energy needs—with billions of dollars of subsidies a year. "Wind isn't commercially feasible with natural gas prices below $6" per thousand cubic feet, notes Mr. Hamm. Right now its price is below $4. This may explain the administration's hostility to the fossil-fuel renaissance.

Mr. Hamm calculates that if Washington would allow more drilling permits for oil and natural gas on federal lands and federal waters, "I truly believe the federal government could over time raise $18 trillion in royalties." That's more than the U.S. national debt, I say. He smiles.

This estimate sounds implausibly high, but Mr. Hamm has a lifelong habit of proving skeptics wrong. And even if he's wrong by half, it's a stunning number to think about. So this America-first energy story isn't just about jobs and economic revival. It's also about repairing America's battered balance sheet. Someone should get this man in front of the congressional deficit-reduction supercommittee.

Mr. Moore is a member of the Journal's editorial board.

Article Index

Additional Readings

The Five Thousand Year Leap, by W. Cleon Skousen

The Naked Communist, by W. Cleon Skousen

The Miracle of America, Audio and Workbook. By W. Cleon Skousen

In CONGRESS, July 4, 1776

The unanimous Declaration of the thirteen united States of America

When in the Course of human events it becomes necessary for one people to dissolve the political bands which have connected them with another and to assume among the powers of the earth, the separate and equal station to which the Laws of Nature and of Nature's God entitle them, a decent respect to the opinions of mankind requires that they should declare the causes which impel them to the separation.

We hold these truths to be self-evident, that all men are created equal, that they are endowed by their Creator with certain unalienable Rights, that among these are Life, Liberty and the pursuit of Happiness. — That to secure these rights, Governments are instituted among Men, deriving their just powers from the consent of the governed, — That whenever any Form of Government becomes destructive of these ends, it is the Right of the People to alter or to abolish it, and to institute new Government, laying its foundation on such principles and organizing its powers in such form, as to them shall seem most likely to effect their Safety and Happiness. Prudence, indeed, will dictate that Governments long established should not be changed for light and transient causes; and accordingly all experience hath shewn that mankind are more disposed to suffer, while evils are sufferable than to right themselves by abolishing the forms to which they are accustomed. But when a long train of abuses and usurpations, pursuing invariably the same Object evinces a design to reduce them under absolute Despotism, it is their right, it is their duty, to throw off such Government, and to provide new Guards for their future security. — Such has been the patient sufferance of these Colonies; and such is now the necessity which constrains them to alter their former Systems of Government. The history of the present King of Great Britain is a history of repeated injuries and usurpations, all having in direct object the establishment of an absolute Tyranny over these States. To prove this, let Facts be submitted to a candid world.

He has refused his Assent to Laws, the most wholesome and necessary for the public good.

He has forbidden his Governors to pass Laws of immediate and pressing importance, unless suspended in their operation till his Assent should be obtained; and when so suspended, he has utterly neglected to attend to them.

He has refused to pass other Laws for the accommodation of large districts of people, unless those people would relinquish the right of Representation in the Legislature, a right inestimable to them and formidable to tyrants only.

He has called together legislative bodies at places unusual, uncomfortable, and distant from the depository of their Public Records, for the sole purpose of fatiguing them into compliance with his measures.

He has dissolved Representative Houses repeatedly, for opposing with manly firmness his invasions on the rights of the people.

He has refused for a long time, after such dissolutions, to cause others to be elected, whereby the Legislative Powers, incapable of Annihilation, have returned to the People at large for their exercise; the State remaining in the mean time exposed to all the dangers of invasion from without, and convulsions within.

He has endeavoured to prevent the population of these States; for that purpose obstructing the Laws for Naturalization of Foreigners; refusing to pass others to encourage their migrations hither, and raising the conditions of new Appropriations of Lands.

He has obstructed the Administration of Justice by refusing his Assent to Laws for establishing Judiciary Powers.

He has made Judges dependent on his Will alone for the tenure of their offices, and the amount and payment of their salaries.

He has erected a multitude of New Offices, and sent hither swarms of Officers to harass our people and eat out their substance.

He has kept among us, in times of peace, Standing Armies without the Consent of our legislatures.

He has affected to render the Military independent of and superior to the Civil Power.

He has combined with others to subject us to a jurisdiction foreign to our constitution, and unacknowledged by our laws; giving his Assent to their Acts of pretended Legislation:

For quartering large bodies of armed troops among us:

For protecting them, by a mock Trial from punishment for any Murders which they should commit on the Inhabitants of these States:

For cutting off our Trade with all parts of the world:

For imposing Taxes on us without our Consent:

For depriving us in many cases, of the benefit of Trial by Jury:

For transporting us beyond Seas to be tried for pretended offences:

For abolishing the free System of English Laws in a neighbouring Province, establishing therein an Arbitrary government, and enlarging its Boundaries so as to render it at once an example and fit instrument for introducing the same absolute rule into these Colonies

For taking away our Charters, abolishing our most valuable Laws and altering fundamentally the Forms of our Governments:

For suspending our own Legislatures, and declaring themselves invested with power to legislate for us in all cases whatsoever.

He has abdicated Government here, by declaring us out of his Protection and waging War against us.

He has plundered our seas, ravaged our coasts, burnt our towns, and destroyed the lives of our people.

He is at this time transporting large Armies of foreign Mercenaries to compleat the works of death, desolation, and tyranny, already begun with circumstances of Cruelty & Perfidy scarcely paralleled in the most barbarous ages, and totally unworthy the Head of a civilized nation.

He has constrained our fellow Citizens taken Captive on the high Seas to bear Arms against their Country, to become the executioners of their friends and Brethren, or to fall themselves by their Hands.

He has excited domestic insurrections amongst us, and has endeavoured to bring on the inhabitants of our frontiers, the merciless Indian Savages whose known rule of warfare, is an undistinguished destruction of all ages, sexes and conditions.

In every stage of these Oppressions We have Petitioned for Redress in the most humble terms: Our repeated Petitions have been answered only by repeated injury. A Prince, whose character is thus marked by every act which may define a Tyrant, is unfit to be the ruler of a free people.

Nor have We been wanting in attentions to our British brethren. We have warned them from time to time of attempts by their legislature to extend an unwarrantable jurisdiction over us. We have reminded them of the circumstances of our emigration and settlement here. We have appealed to their native justice and magnanimity, and we have conjured them by the ties of our common kindred to disavow these usurpations, which would inevitably interrupt our connections and correspondence. They too have been deaf to the voice of justice and of consanguinity. We must, therefore, acquiesce in the necessity, which denounces our Separation, and hold them, as we hold the rest of mankind, Enemies in War, in Peace Friends.

We, therefore, the Representatives of the united States of America, in General Congress, Assembled, appealing to the Supreme Judge of the world for the rectitude of our intentions, do, in the Name, and by Authority of the good People of these Colonies, solemnly publish and declare, That these united Colonies are, and of Right ought to be Free and Independent States, that they are Absolved from all Allegiance to the British Crown, and that all political connection between them and the State of Great Britain, is and ought to be totally dissolved; and that as Free and Independent States, they have full Power to levy War, conclude Peace, contract Alliances, establish Commerce, and to do all other Acts and Things which Independent States may of right do. — And for the support of this Declaration, with a firm reliance on the protection of Divine Providence, we mutually pledge to each other our Lives, our Fortunes, and our sacred Honor.

— John Hancock

New Hampshire:
Josiah Bartlett, William Whipple, Matthew Thornton

Massachusetts:
John Hancock, Samuel Adams, John Adams, Robert Treat Paine, Elbridge Gerry

Rhode Island:
Stephen Hopkins, William Ellery

Connecticut:
Roger Sherman, Samuel Huntington, William Williams, Oliver Wolcott

New York:

William Floyd, Philip Livingston, Francis Lewis, Lewis Morris

New Jersey:

Richard Stockton, John Witherspoon, Francis Hopkinson, John Hart, Abraham Clark

Pennsylvania:

Robert Morris, Benjamin Rush, Benjamin Franklin, John Morton, George Clymer, James Smith, George Taylor, James Wilson, George Ross

Delaware:

Caesar Rodney, George Read, Thomas McKean

Maryland:

Samuel Chase, William Paca, Thomas Stone, Charles Carroll of Carrollton

Virginia:

George Wythe, Richard Henry Lee, Thomas Jefferson, Benjamin Harrison, Thomas Nelson, Jr., Francis Lightfoot Lee, Carter Braxton

North Carolina:

William Hooper, Joseph Hewes, John Penn

South Carolina:

Edward Rutledge, Thomas Heyward, Jr., Thomas Lynch, Jr., Arthur Middleton

Georgia:

Button Gwinnett, Lyman Hall, George Walton

THE CONSTITUTION OF THE UNITED STATES OF AMERICA

We the People of the United States, in Order to form a more perfect Union, establish Justice, insure domestic Tranquility, provide for the common defence, promote the general Welfare, and secure the Blessings of Liberty toourselves and our Posterity, do ordain and establish this Constitution for the United States of America.

Article 1.

Section 1
All legislative Powers herein granted shall be vested in a Congress of the United States, which shall consist of a Senate and House of Representatives.

Section 2
The House of Representatives shall be composed of Members chosen every second Year by the People of the several States, and the Electors in each State shall have the Qualifications requisite for Electors of the most numerous Branch of the State Legislature.

No Person shall be a Representative who shall not have attained to the Age of twenty five Years, and been seven Years a Citizen of the United States, and who shall not, when elected, be an Inhabitant of that State in which he shall be chosen.

Representatives and direct Taxes shall be apportioned among the several States which may be included within this Union, according to their respective Numbers, which shall be determined by adding to the whole Number of free Persons, including those bound to Service for a Term of Years, and excluding Indians not taxed, three fifths of all other Persons.

The actual Enumeration shall be made within three Years after the first Meeting of the Congress of the United States, and within every subsequent Term of ten Years, in such Manner as they shall by Law direct. The Number of Representatives shall not exceed one for every thirty Thousand, but each State shall have at Least one Representative; and until such enumeration shall be made, the State of New Hampshire shall be entitled to choose three, Massachusetts eight, Rhode Island and Providence Plantations one, Connecticut five, New York six, New Jersey four, Pennsylvania eight, Delaware one, Maryland six, Virginia ten, North Carolina five, South Carolina five and Georgia three.

When vacancies happen in the Representation from any State, the Executive Authority thereof shall issue Writs of Election to fill such Vacancies.

The House of Representatives shall choose their Speaker and other Officers; and shall have the sole Power of Impeachment.

Section 3
The Senate of the United States shall be composed of two Senators from each State, chosen by the Legislature thereof, for six Years; and each Senator shall have one Vote.

Immediately after they shall be assembled in Consequence of the first Election, they shall be divided as equally as may be into three Classes. The Seats of the Senators of the first Class shall be vacated at the Expiration of the second Year, of the second Class at the Expiration of the fourth Year, and of the third Class at the Expiration of the sixth Year, so that one third may be chosen every second Year; and if Vacancies happen by Resignation, or otherwise, during the Recess of the Legislature of any State, the Executive thereof may make temporary Appointments until the next Meeting of the Legislature, which shall then fill such Vacancies.

No person shall be a Senator who shall not have attained to the Age of thirty Years, and been nine Years a Citizen of the United States, and who shall not, when elected, be an Inhabitant of that State for which he shall be chosen.

The Vice President of the United States shall be President of the Senate, but shall have no Vote, unless they be equally divided.

The Senate shall choose their other Officers, and also a President pro tempore, in the absence of the Vice President, or when he shall exercise the Office of President of the United States.

The Senate shall have the sole Power to try all Impeachments. When sitting for that Purpose, they shall be on Oath or Affirmation. When the President of the United States is tried, the Chief Justice shall preside: And no Person shall be convicted without the Concurrence of two thirds of the Members present.

Judgment in Cases of Impeachment shall not extend further than to removal from Office, and disqualification to hold and enjoy any Office of honor, Trust or Profit under the United States: but the Party convicted shall nevertheless be liable and subject to Indictment, Trial, Judgment and Punishment, according to Law.

Section 4

The Times, Places and Manner of holding Elections for Senators and Representatives, shall be prescribed in each State by the Legislature thereof; but the Congress may at any time by Law make or alter such Regulations, except as to the Place of Choosing Senators.

The Congress shall assemble at least once in every Year, and such Meeting shall be on the first Monday in December, unless they shall by Law appoint a different Day.

Section 5

Each House shall be the Judge of the Elections, Returns and Qualifications of its own Members, and a Majority of each shall constitute a Quorum to do Business; but a smaller number may adjourn from day to day, and may be authorized to compel the Attendance of absent Members, in such Manner, and under such Penalties as each House may provide.

Each House may determine the Rules of its Proceedings, punish its Members for disorderly Behavior, and, with the Concurrence of two-thirds, expel a Member.

Each House shall keep a Journal of its Proceedings, and from time to time publish the same, excepting such Parts as may in their Judgment require Secrecy; and the Yeas and Nays of the Members of either House on any question shall, at the Desire of one fifth of those Present, be entered on the Journal.

Neither House, during the Session of Congress, shall, without the Consent of the other, adjourn for more than three days, nor to any other Place than that in which the two Houses shall be sitting.

Section 6

The Senators and Representatives shall receive a Compensation for their Services, to be ascertained by Law, and paid out of the

Treasury of the United States. They shall in all Cases, except Treason, Felony and Breach of the Peace, be privileged from Arrest during their Attendance at the Session of their respective Houses, and in going to and returning from the same; and for any Speech or Debate in either House, they shall not be questioned in any other Place.

No Senator or Representative shall, during the Time for which he was elected, be appointed to any civil Office under the Authority of the United States which shall have been created, or the Emoluments whereof shall have been increased during such time; and no Person holding any Office under the United States, shall be a Member of either House during his Continuance in Office.

Section 7
All bills for raising Revenue shall originate in the House of Representatives; but the Senate may propose or concur with Amendments as on other Bills.

Every Bill which shall have passed the House of Representatives and the Senate, shall, before it become a Law, be presented to the President of the United States; If he approve he shall sign it, but if not he shall return it, with his Objections to that House in which it shall have originated, who shall enter the Objections at large on their Journal, and proceed to reconsider it. If after such Reconsideration two thirds of that House shall agree to pass the Bill, it shall be sent, together with the Objections, to the other House, by which it shall likewise be reconsidered, and if approved by two thirds of that House, it shall become a Law. But in all such Cases the Votes of both Houses shall be determined by Yeas and Nays, and the Names of the Persons voting for and against the Bill shall be entered on the Journal of each House respectively. If any Bill shall not be returned by the President within ten Days (Sundays excepted) after it shall have been presented to him, the same shall be a Law, in like Manner as if he had signed it, unless the Congress by their Adjournment prevent its Return, in which Case it shall not be a Law.

Every Order, Resolution, or Vote to which the Concurrence of the Senate and House of Representatives may be necessary (except on a question of Adjournment) shall be presented to the President of the United States; and before the Same shall take Effect, shall be approved by him, or being disapproved by him, shall be repassed by two thirds of the Senate and House of Representatives, according to the Rules and Limitations prescribed in the Case of a Bill.

Section 8

The Congress shall have Power To lay and collect Taxes, Duties, Imposts and Excises, to pay the Debts and provide for the common Defence and general Welfare of the United States; but all Duties, Imposts and Excises shall be uniform throughout the United States;

To borrow money on the credit of the United States;

To regulate Commerce with foreign Nations, and among the several States, and with the Indian Tribes;

To establish an uniform Rule of Naturalization, and uniform Laws on the subject of Bankruptcies throughout the United States;

To coin Money, regulate the Value thereof, and of foreign Coin, and fix the Standard of Weights and Measures;

To provide for the Punishment of counterfeiting the Securities and current Coin of the United States;

To establish Post Offices and Post Roads;

To promote the Progress of Science and useful Arts, by securing for limited Times to Authors and Inventors the exclusive Right to their respective Writings and Discoveries;

To constitute Tribunals inferior to the supreme Court;

To define and punish Piracies and Felonies committed on the high Seas, and Offenses against the Law of Nations;

To declare War, grant Letters of Marque and Reprisal, and make Rules concerning Captures on Land and Water;

To raise and support Armies, but no Appropriation of Money to that Use shall be for a longer Term than two Years;

To provide and maintain a Navy;

To make Rules for the Government and Regulation of the land and naval Forces;

To provide for calling forth the Militia to execute the Laws of the Union, suppress Insurrections and repel Invasions;

To provide for organizing, arming, and disciplining, the Militia, and for governing such Part of them as may be employed in the Service of the United States, reserving to the States respectively, the Appointment of the Officers, and the Authority of training the Militia according to the discipline prescribed by Congress;

To exercise exclusive Legislation in all Cases whatsoever, over such District (not exceeding ten Miles square) as may, by Cession of particular States, and the acceptance of Congress, become the Seat of the Government of the United States, and to exercise like Authority over all Places purchased by the Consent of the Legislature of the State in which the Same shall be, for the

Erection of Forts, Magazines, Arsenals, dock-Yards, and other needful Buildings; And

To make all Laws which shall be necessary and proper for carrying into Execution the foregoing Powers, and all other Powers vested by this Constitution in the Government of the United States, or in any Department or Officer thereof.

Section 9

The Migration or Importation of such Persons as any of the States now existing shall think proper to admit, shall not be prohibited by the Congress prior to the Year one thousand eight hundred and eight, but a tax or duty may be imposed on such Importation, not exceeding ten dollars for each Person.

The privilege of the Writ of Habeas Corpus shall not be suspended, unless when in Cases of Rebellion or Invasion the public Safety may require it.

No Bill of Attainder or ex post facto Law shall be passed.

No capitation, or other direct, Tax shall be laid, unless in Proportion to the Census or Enumeration herein before directed to be taken.

No Tax or Duty shall be laid on Articles exported from any State. No Preference shall be given by any Regulation of Commerce or Revenue to the Ports of one State over those of another: nor shall Vessels bound to, or from, one State, be obliged to enter, clear, or pay Duties in another.

No Money shall be drawn from the Treasury, but in Consequence of Appropriations made by Law; and a regular Statement and Account of the Receipts and Expenditures of all public Money shall be published from time to time.

No Title of Nobility shall be granted by the United States: And no Person holding any Office of Profit or Trust under them, shall, without the Consent of the Congress, accept of any present, Emolument, Office, or Title, of any kind whatever, from any King, Prince or foreign State.

Section 10

No State shall enter into any Treaty, Alliance, or Confederation; grant Letters of Marque and Reprisal; coin Money; emit Bills of Credit; make any Thing but gold and silver Coin a Tender in Payment of Debts; pass any Bill of Attainder, ex post facto Law, or Law impairing the Obligation of Contracts, or grant any Title of Nobility.

No State shall, without the Consent of the Congress, lay any Imposts or Duties on Imports or Exports, except what may be absolutely necessary for executing its inspection Laws: and the net Produce of all Duties and Imposts, laid by any State on Imports or Exports, shall be for the Use of the Treasury of the United States; and all such Laws shall be subject to the Revision and Control of the Congress.

No State shall, without the Consent of Congress, lay any duty of Tonnage, keep Troops, or Ships of War in time of Peace, enter into any Agreement or Compact with another State, or with a foreign Power, or engage in War, unless actually invaded, or in such imminent Danger as will not admit of delay.

Article 2.

Section 1

The executive Power shall be vested in a President of the United States of America. He shall hold his Office during the Term of four Years, and, together with the Vice-President chosen for the same Term, be elected, as follows:

Each State shall appoint, in such Manner as the Legislature thereof may direct, a Number of Electors, equal to the whole Number of Senators and Representatives to which the State may be entitled in the Congress: but no Senator or Representative, or Person holding an Office of Trust or Profit under the United States, shall be appointed an Elector.

The Electors shall meet in their respective States, and vote by Ballot for two persons, of whom one at least shall not lie an Inhabitant of the same State with themselves. And they shall make a List of all the Persons voted for, and of the Number of Votes for each; which List they shall sign and certify, and transmit sealed to the Seat of the Government of the United States, directed to the President of the Senate. The President of the Senate shall, in the Presence of the Senate and House of Representatives, open all the Certificates, and the Votes shall then be counted. The Person having the greatest Number of Votes shall be the President, if such Number be a Majority of the whole Number of Electors appointed; and if there be more than one who have such Majority, and have an equal Number of Votes, then the House of Representatives shall immediately choose by Ballot one of them for President; and if no Person have a Majority, then from the five highest on the List the said House shall in like Manner choose the President. But in choosing the President, the Votes shall be taken by States, the Representation from each State having one Vote; a quorum for this Purpose shall consist of a Member or Members from two-thirds of the States, and a Majority of all the States shall be necessary to a Choice. In every Case, after the Choice of the President, the Person having the greatest Number of Votes of the Electors shall be the Vice President. But if there should remain two or more who have equal Votes, the Senate shall choose from them by Ballot the Vice-President.

The Congress may determine the Time of choosing the Electors, and the Day on which they shall give their Votes; which Day shall be the same throughout the United States.

No person except a natural born Citizen, or a Citizen of the United States, at the time of the Adoption of this Constitution, shall be eligible to the Office of President; neither shall any Person be eligible to that Office who shall not have attained to the Age of thirty-five Years, and been fourteen Years a Resident within the United States.

In Case of the Removal of the President from Office, or of his Death, Resignation, or Inability to discharge the Powers and Duties of the said Office, the same shall devolve on the Vice President, and the Congress may by Law provide for the Case of Removal, Death, Resignation or Inability, both of the President and Vice President, declaring what Officer shall then act as President, and such Officer shall act accordingly, until the Disability be removed, or a President shall be elected.

The President shall, at stated Times, receive for his Services, a Compensation, which shall neither be increased nor diminished during the Period for which he shall have been elected, and he shall not receive within that Period any other Emolument from the United States, or any of them.

Before he enter on the Execution of his Office, he shall take the following Oath or Affirmation:

"I do solemnly swear (or affirm) that I will faithfully execute the Office of President of the United States, and will to the best of my Ability, preserve, protect and defend the Constitution of the United States."

Section 2
The President shall be Commander in Chief of the Army and Navy of the United States, and of the Militia of the several States, when called into the actual Service of the United States; he may require the Opinion, in writing, of the principal Officer in each

of the executive Departments, upon any subject relating to the Duties of their respective Offices, and he shall have Power to Grant Reprieves and Pardons for Offenses against the United States, except in Cases of Impeachment.

He shall have Power, by and with the Advice and Consent of the Senate, to make Treaties, provided two thirds of the Senators present concur; and he shall nominate, and by and with the Advice and Consent of the Senate, shall appoint Ambassadors, other public Ministers and Consuls, Judges of the supreme Court, and all other Officers of the United States, whose Appointments are not herein otherwise provided for, and which shall be established by Law: but the Congress may by Law vest the Appointment of such inferior Officers, as they think proper, in the President alone, in the Courts of Law, or in the Heads of Departments.

The President shall have Power to fill up all Vacancies that may happen during the Recess of the Senate, by granting Commissions which shall expire at the End of their next Session.

Section 3
He shall from time to time give to the Congress Information of the State of the Union, and recommend to their Consideration such Measures as he shall judge necessary and expedient; he may, on extraordinary Occasions, convene both Houses, or either of them, and in Case of Disagreement between them, with Respect to the Time of Adjournment, he may adjourn them to such Time as he shall think proper; he shall receive Ambassadors and other public Ministers; he shall take Care that the Laws be faithfully executed, and shall Commission all the Officers of the United States.

Section 4
The President, Vice President and all civil Officers of the United States, shall be removed from Office on Impeachment for,

and Conviction of, Treason, Bribery, or other high Crimes and Misdemeanors.

Article 3.

Section 1

The judicial Power of the United States, shall be vested in one supreme Court, and in such inferior Courts as the Congress may from time to time ordain and establish. The Judges, both of the supreme and inferior Courts, shall hold their Offices during good Behavior, and shall, at stated Times, receive for their Services a Compensation which shall not be diminished during their Continuance in Office.

Section 2

The judicial Power shall extend to all Cases, in Law and Equity, arising under this Constitution, the Laws of the United States, and Treaties made, or which shall be made, under their Authority; to all Cases affecting Ambassadors, other public Ministers and Consuls; to all Cases of admiralty and maritime Jurisdiction; to Controversies to which the United States shall be a Party; to Controversies between two or more States; between a State and Citizens of another State; between Citizens of different States; between Citizens of the same State claiming Lands under Grants of different States, and between a State, or the Citizens thereof, and foreign States, Citizens or Subjects.

In all Cases affecting Ambassadors, other public Ministers and Consuls, and those in which a State shall be Party, the supreme Court shall have original Jurisdiction. In all the other Cases before mentioned, the supreme Court shall have appellate Jurisdiction, both as to Law and Fact, with such Exceptions, and under such Regulations as the Congress shall make.

The Trial of all Crimes, except in Cases of Impeachment, shall be by Jury; and such Trial shall be held in the State where the said Crimes shall have been committed; but when not committed within any State, the Trial shall be at such Place or Places as the Congress may by Law have directed.

Section 3
Treason against the United States, shall consist only in levying War against them, or in adhering to their Enemies, giving them Aid and Comfort. No Person shall be convicted of Treason unless on the Testimony of two Witnesses to the same overt Act, or on Confession in open Court.

The Congress shall have power to declare the Punishment of Treason, but no Attainder of Treason shall work Corruption of Blood, or Forfeiture except during the Life of the Person attainted.

Article 4.

Section 1
Full Faith and Credit shall be given in each State to the public Acts, Records, and judicial Proceedings of every other State. And the Congress may by general Laws prescribe the Manner in which such Acts, Records and Proceedings shall be proved, and the Effect thereof.

Section 2
The Citizens of each State shall be entitled to all Privileges and Immunities of Citizens in the several States.

A Person charged in any State with Treason, Felony, or other Crime, who shall flee from Justice, and be found in another State, shall on demand of the executive Authority of the State from which he fled, be delivered up, to be removed to the State having Jurisdiction of the Crime.

No Person held to Service or Labour in one State, under the Laws thereof, escaping into another, shall, in Consequence of any Law or Regulation therein, be discharged from such Service or Labour, But shall be delivered up on Claim of the Party to whom such Service or Labour may be due.

Section 3

New States may be admitted by the Congress into this Union; but no new States shall be formed or erected within the Jurisdiction of any other State; nor any State be formed by the Junction of two or more States, or parts of States, without the Consent of the Legislatures of the States concerned as well as of the Congress.

The Congress shall have Power to dispose of and make all needful Rules and Regulations respecting the Territory or other Property belonging to the United States; and nothing in this Constitution shall be so construed as to Prejudice any Claims of the United States, or of any particular State.

Section 4

The United States shall guarantee to every State in this Union a Republican Form of Government, and shall protect each of them against Invasion; and on Application of the Legislature, or of the Executive (when the Legislature cannot be convened) against domestic Violence.

Article 5.

The Congress, whenever two thirds of both Houses shall deem it necessary, shall propose Amendments to this Constitution, or, on the Application of the Legislatures of two thirds of the several States, shall call a Convention for proposing Amendments, which, in either Case, shall be valid to all Intents and Purposes, as part of this Constitution, when ratified by the Legislatures of three fourths of the several States, or by Conventions in three fourths thereof, as the one or the other Mode of Ratification may be proposed by the Congress; Provided that no Amendment which may be made prior to the Year One thousand eight hundred and eight shall in any Manner affect the first and fourth Clauses in the Ninth Section of the first Article; and that no State, without its Consent, shall be deprived of its equal Suffrage in the Senate.

Article 6.

All Debts contracted and Engagements entered into, before the Adoption of this Constitution, shall be as valid against the United States under this Constitution, as under the Confederation.

This Constitution, and the Laws of the United States which shall be made in Pursuance thereof; and all Treaties made, or which shall be made, under the Authority of the United States, shall be the supreme Law of the Land; and the Judges in every State shall be bound thereby, any Thing in the Constitution or Laws of any State to the Contrary notwithstanding.

The Senators and Representatives before mentioned, and the Members of the several State Legislatures, and all executive and judicial Officers, both of the United States and of the several States, shall be bound by Oath or Affirmation, to support this Constitution; but no religious Test shall ever be required as a Qualification to any Office or public Trust under the United States.

Article 7.

The Ratification of the Conventions of nine States, shall be sufficient for the Establishment of this Constitution between the States so ratifying the Same.

Done in Convention by the Unanimous Consent of the States present the Seventeenth Day of September in the Year of our

Lord one thousand seven hundred and Eighty seven and of the Independence of the United States of America the Twelfth. In Witness whereof We have hereunto subscribed our Names.

George Washington - President and deputy from Virginia

New Hampshire - John Langdon, Nicholas Gilman

Massachusetts - Nathaniel Gorham, Rufus King

Connecticut - William Samuel Johnson, Roger Sherman

New York - Alexander Hamilton

New Jersey - William Livingston, David Brearley, William Paterson, Jonathan Dayton

Pennsylvania - Benjamin Franklin, Thomas Mifflin, Robert Morris, George Clymer, Thomas Fitzsimons, Jared Ingersoll, James Wilson, Gouvernour Morris

Delaware - George Read, Gunning Bedford Jr., John Dickinson, Richard Bassett, Jacob Broom

Maryland - James McHenry, Daniel of St Thomas Jenifer, Daniel Carroll

Virginia - John Blair, James Madison Jr.

North Carolina - William Blount, Richard Dobbs Spaight, Hugh Williamson

South Carolina - John Rutledge, Charles Cotesworth Pinckney, Charles Pinckney, Pierce Butler

Georgia - William Few, Abraham Baldwin

Attest: William Jackson, Secretary

Amendment 1
Congress shall make no law respecting an establishment of religion, or prohibiting the free exercise thereof; or abridging the freedom of speech, or of the press; or the right of the people peaceably to assemble, and to petition the Government for a redress of grievances.

Amendment 2
A well regulated Militia, being necessary to the security of a free State, the right of the people to keep and bear Arms, shall not be infringed.

Amendment 3
No Soldier shall, in time of peace be quartered in any house, without the consent of the Owner, nor in time of war, but in a manner to be prescribed by law.

Amendment 4
The right of the people to be secure in their persons, houses, papers, and effects, against unreasonable searches and seizures, shall not be violated, and no Warrants shall issue, but upon probable cause, supported by Oath or affirmation, and particularly describing the place to be searched, and the persons or things to be seized.

Amendment 5
No person shall be held to answer for a capital, or otherwise infamous crime, unless on a presentment or indictment of a Grand Jury, except in cases arising in the land or naval forces, or in the Militia, when in actual service in time of War or public danger; nor shall any person be subject for the same offense to

be twice put in jeopardy of life or limb; nor shall be compelled in any criminal case to be a witness against himself, nor be deprived of life, liberty, or property, without due process of law; nor shall private property be taken for public use, without just compensation.

Amendment 6
In all criminal prosecutions, the accused shall enjoy the right to a speedy and public trial, by an impartial jury of the State and district wherein the crime shall have been committed, which district shall have been previously ascertained by law, and to be informed of the nature and cause of the accusation; to be confronted with the witnesses against him; to have compulsory process for obtaining witnesses in his favor, and to have the Assistance of Counsel for his defence.

Amendment 7
In Suits at common law, where the value in controversy shall exceed twenty dollars, the right of trial by jury shall be preserved, and no fact tried by a jury, shall be otherwise re-examined in any Court of the United States, than according to the rules of the common law.

Amendment 8
Excessive bail shall not be required, nor excessive fines imposed, nor cruel and unusual punishments inflicted.

Amendment 9
The enumeration in the Constitution, of certain rights, shall not be construed to deny or disparage others retained by the people.

Amendment 10
The powers not delegated to the United States by the Constitution, nor prohibited by it to the States, are reserved to the States respectively, or to the people.

Amendment 11

The Judicial power of the United States shall not be construed to extend to any suit in law or equity, commenced or prosecuted against one of the United States by Citizens of another State, or by Citizens or Subjects of any Foreign State.

Amendment 12

The Electors shall meet in their respective states, and vote by ballot for President and Vice-President, one of whom, at least, shall not be an inhabitant of the same state with themselves; they shall name in their ballots the person voted for as President, and in distinct ballots the person voted for as Vice-President, and they shall make distinct lists of all persons voted for as President, and of all persons voted for as Vice-President and of the number of votes for each, which lists they shall sign and certify, and transmit sealed to the seat of the government of the United States, directed to the President of the Senate; The President of the Senate shall, in the presence of the Senate and House of Representatives, open all the certificates and the votes shall then be counted;

The person having the greatest Number of votes for President, shall be the President, if such number be a majority of the whole number of Electors appointed; and if no person have such majority, then from the persons having the highest numbers not exceeding three on the list of those voted for as President, the House of Representatives shall choose immediately, by ballot, the President. But in choosing the President, the votes shall be taken by states, the representation from each state having one vote; a quorum for this purpose shall consist of a member or members from two-thirds of the states, and a majority of all the states shall be necessary to a choice. And if the House of Representatives shall not choose a President whenever the right of choice shall devolve upon them, before the fourth day of March next following, then the Vice-President shall act as President, as in the case of the death or other constitutional disability of the President.

The person having the greatest number of votes as Vice-President, shall be the Vice-President, if such number be a majority of the whole number of Electors appointed, and if no person have a majority, then from the two highest numbers on the list, the Senate shall choose the Vice-President; a quorum for the purpose shall consist of two-thirds of the whole number of Senators, and a majority of the whole number shall be necessary to a choice. But no person constitutionally ineligible to the office of President shall be eligible to that of Vice-President of the United States.

Amendment 13
1. Neither slavery nor involuntary servitude, except as a punishment for crime whereof the party shall have been duly convicted, shall exist within the United States, or any place subject to their jurisdiction.

2. Congress shall have power to enforce this article by appropriate legislation.

Amendment 14
1. All persons born or naturalized in the United States, and subject to the jurisdiction thereof, are citizens of the United States and of the State wherein they reside. No State shall make or enforce any law which shall abridge the privileges or immunities of citizens of the United States; nor shall any State deprive any person of life, liberty, or property, without due process of law; nor deny to any person within its jurisdiction the equal protection of the laws.

2. Representatives shall be apportioned among the several States according to their respective numbers, counting the whole number of persons in each State, excluding Indians not taxed. But when the right to vote at any election for the choice of electors for President and Vice-President of the United States, Representatives in Congress, the Executive and Judicial officers

of a State, or the members of the Legislature thereof, is denied to any of the male inhabitants of such State, being twenty-one years of age, and citizens of the United States, or in any way abridged, except for participation in rebellion, or other crime, the basis of representation therein shall be reduced in the proportion which the number of such male citizens shall bear to the whole number of male citizens twenty-one years of age in such State.

3. No person shall be a Senator or Representative in Congress, or elector of President and Vice-President, or hold any office, civil or military, under the United States, or under any State, who, having previously taken an oath, as a member of Congress, or as an officer of the United States, or as a member of any State legislature, or as an executive or judicial officer of any State, to support the Constitution of the United States, shall have engaged in insurrection or rebellion against the same, or given aid or comfort to the enemies thereof. But Congress may by a vote of two-thirds of each House, remove such disability.

4. The validity of the public debt of the United States, authorized by law, including debts incurred for payment of pensions and bounties for services in suppressing insurrection or rebellion, shall not be questioned. But neither the United States nor any State shall assume or pay any debt or obligation incurred in aid of insurrection or rebellion against the United States, or any claim for the loss or emancipation of any slave; but all such debts, obligations and claims shall be held illegal and void.

5. The Congress shall have power to enforce, by appropriate legislation, the provisions of this article.

Amendment 15
1. The right of citizens of the United States to vote shall not be denied or abridged by the United States or by any State on account of race, color, or previous condition of servitude.

2. The Congress shall have power to enforce this article by appropriate legislation.

Amendment 16
The Congress shall have power to lay and collect taxes on incomes, from whatever source derived, without apportionment among the several States, and without regard to any census or enumeration.

Amendment 17
The Senate of the United States shall be composed of two Senators from each State, elected by the people thereof, for six years; and each Senator shall have one vote. The electors in each State shall have the qualifications requisite for electors of the most numerous branch of the State legislatures.

When vacancies happen in the representation of any State in the Senate, the executive authority of such State shall issue writs of election to fill such vacancies: Provided, That the legislature of any State may empower the executive thereof to make temporary appointments until the people fill the vacancies by election as the legislature may direct.

This amendment shall not be so construed as to affect the election or term of any Senator chosen before it becomes valid as part of the Constitution.

Amendment 18
1. After one year from the ratification of this article the manufacture, sale, or transportation of intoxicating liquors within, the importation thereof into, or the exportation thereof from the United States and all territory subject to the jurisdiction thereof for beverage purposes is hereby prohibited.

2. The Congress and the several States shall have concurrent power to enforce this article by appropriate legislation.

3. This article shall be inoperative unless it shall have been ratified as an amendment to the Constitution by the legislatures of the several States, as provided in the Constitution, within seven years from the date of the submission hereof to the States by the Congress.

Amendment 19
The right of citizens of the United States to vote shall not be denied or abridged by the United States or by any State on account of sex.

Congress shall have power to enforce this article by appropriate legislation.

Amendment 20
1. The terms of the President and Vice President shall end at noon on the 20th day of January, and the terms of Senators and Representatives at noon on the 3d day of January, of the years in which such terms would have ended if this article had not been ratified; and the terms of their successors shall then begin.

2. The Congress shall assemble at least once in every year, and such meeting shall begin at noon on the 3d day of January, unless they shall by law appoint a different day.

3. If, at the time fixed for the beginning of the term of the President, the President elect shall have died, the Vice President elect shall become President. If a President shall not have been chosen before the time fixed for the beginning of his term, or if the President elect shall have failed to qualify, then the Vice President elect shall act as President until a President shall have qualified; and the Congress may by law provide for the

case wherein neither a President elect nor a Vice President elect shall have qualified, declaring who shall then act as President, or the manner in which one who is to act shall be selected, and such person shall act accordingly until a President or Vice President shall have qualified.

4. The Congress may by law provide for the case of the death of any of the persons from whom the House of Representatives may choose a President whenever the right of choice shall have devolved upon them, and for the case of the death of any of the persons from whom the Senate may choose a Vice President whenever the right of choice shall have devolved upon them.

5. Sections 1 and 2 shall take effect on the 15th day of October following the ratification of this article.

6. This article shall be inoperative unless it shall have been ratified as an amendment to the Constitution by the legislatures of three-fourths of the several States within seven years from the date of its submission.

Amendment 21
1. The eighteenth article of amendment to the Constitution of the United States is hereby repealed.

2. The transportation or importation into any State, Territory, or possession of the United States for delivery or use therein of intoxicating liquors, in violation of the laws thereof, is hereby prohibited.

3. The article shall be inoperative unless it shall have been ratified as an amendment to the Constitution by conventions in the several States, as provided in the Constitution, within seven years from the date of the submission hereof to the States by the Congress.

Amendment 22

1. No person shall be elected to the office of the President more than twice, and no person who has held the office of President, or acted as President, for more than two years of a term to which some other person was elected President shall be elected to the office of the President more than once. But this Article shall not apply to any person holding the office of President, when this Article was proposed by the Congress, and shall not prevent any person who may be holding the office of President, or acting as President, during the term within which this Article becomes operative from holding the office of President or acting as President during the remainder of such term.

2. This article shall be inoperative unless it shall have been ratified as an amendment to the Constitution by the legislatures of three-fourths of the several States within seven years from the date of its submission to the States by the Congress.

Amendment 23

1. The District constituting the seat of Government of the United States shall appoint in such manner as the Congress may direct: A number of electors of President and Vice President equal to the whole number of Senators and Representatives in Congress to which the District would be entitled if it were a State, but in no event more than the least populous State; they shall be in addition to those appointed by the States, but they shall be considered, for the purposes of the election of President and Vice President, to be electors appointed by a State; and they shall meet in the District and perform such duties as provided by the twelfth article of amendment.

2. The Congress shall have power to enforce this article by appropriate legislation.

Amendment 24
1. The right of citizens of the United States to vote in any primary or other election for President or Vice President, for electors for President or Vice President, or for Senator or Representative in Congress, shall not be denied or abridged by the United States or any State by reason of failure to pay any poll tax or other tax.

2. The Congress shall have power to enforce this article by appropriate legislation.

Amendment 25
1. In case of the removal of the President from office or of his death or resignation, the Vice President shall become President.

2. Whenever there is a vacancy in the office of the Vice President, the President shall nominate a Vice President who shall take office upon confirmation by a majority vote of both Houses of Congress.

3. Whenever the President transmits to the President pro tempore of the Senate and the Speaker of the House of Representatives his written declaration that he is unable to discharge the powers and duties of his office, and until he transmits to them a written declaration to the contrary, such powers and duties shall be discharged by the Vice President as Acting President.

4. Whenever the Vice President and a majority of either the principal officers of the executive departments or of such other body as Congress may by law provide, transmit to the President pro tempore of the Senate and the Speaker of the House of Representatives their written declaration that the President is unable to discharge the powers and duties of his office, the Vice President shall immediately assume the powers and duties of the office as Acting President.

Thereafter, when the President transmits to the President pro tempore of the Senate and the Speaker of the House of Representatives his written declaration that no inability exists, he shall resume the powers and duties of his office unless the Vice President and a majority of either the principal officers of the executive department or of such other body as Congress may by law provide, transmit within four days to the President pro tempore of the Senate and the Speaker of the House of Representatives their written declaration that the President is unable to discharge the powers and duties of his office. Thereupon Congress shall decide the issue, assembling within forty eight hours for that purpose if not in session. If the Congress, within twenty one days after receipt of the latter written declaration, or, if Congress is not in session, within twenty one days after Congress is required to assemble, determines by two thirds vote of both Houses that the President is unable to discharge the powers and duties of his office, the Vice President shall continue to discharge the same as Acting President; otherwise, the President shall resume the powers and duties of his office.

Amendment 26
1. The right of citizens of the United States, who are eighteen years of age or older, to vote shall not be denied or abridged by the United States or by any State on account of age.

2. The Congress shall have power to enforce this article by appropriate legislation.

Amendment 27
No law, varying the compensation for the services of the Senators and Representatives, shall take effect, until an election of Representatives shall have intervened.

www.ingramcontent.com/pod-product-compliance
Lightning Source LLC
Chambersburg PA
CBHW060302290526
45789CB00001B/387